"The Word of the Lord"

"The Word of the Lord"

Liturgy's Use of Scripture

David N. Power, O.M.I.

ORBIS BOOKS

Maryknoll, New York 10545

Acknowledgment is hereby made to Persea Books, New York, for use of the citation on page 110 of lines from "Tübingen, January," by Paul Celan, taken from *Poems of Paul Celan,* translated by Michael Hamburger; and to Bayleaf Publications, Dublin, for use of the citation on page 70 of lines from "The Collapse of Morality?" by Brian Power, taken from *The Past Must Rise: Poems by Brian Power.*

Founded in 1970, Orbis Books endeavors to publish works that enlighten the mind, nourish the spirit, and challenge the conscience. The publishing arm of the Maryknoll Fathers and Brothers, Orbis seeks to explore the global dimensions of the Christian faith and mission, to invite dialogue with diverse cultures and religious traditions, and to serve the cause of reconciliation and peace. The books published reflect the views of their authors and do not represent the official position of the Society. To learn more about Maryknoll and Orbis Books, please visit our website at www.maryknoll.com.

Manufactured in the United States of America

Library of Congress Cataloging-in-Publication Data
Power, David Noel.
    The Word of the Lord : liturgy's use of scripture / David N. Power.
      p. cm.
    Includes bibliographical information and index.
    ISBN 1-57075-397-0
    1. Bible – Liturgical use. I. Title.
  BS538.3 P69 2001
  264'.34 – dc21

                                    2001036469

Contents

Part Two
OF SCRIPTURES, PRAYERS,
AND ROOT METAPHORS

Preface

The Issue

WHEN CHRISTIAN CONGREGATIONS meet for worship, the proclamation of the scriptures as the Word of God is of the essence. An abundant, if selective, use is made of them, in particular seasons and throughout the calendar year. The faithful of our churches today are often well versed in a knowledge of the Bible and its books, and with this deeper knowledge are ready both to reflect on the texts and to query their use. New prayer texts have been formulated, and one of the tests of their adequacy is how congruent they are with the scriptural Word and imagery.

On the other hand, it is not that clear what is intended by presenting scriptural texts as the Word of God. It is not a reading of the text itself in its original composition and context which is offered but its proclamation in a community of faith, with an orientation to liturgical ritual and prayer. What then is in fact being done with the texts?

Various trends in literary and in biblical hermeneutics have something to say to our understanding of how scriptural texts are chosen, proclaimed, interpreted, and received. The technical vocabulary of this field of inquiry and theory can be obscure. Is it possible to address the concerns which it raises and to address them within our congregations, without resorting to technical terms or convoluted argumentation, while not oversimplifying what is at stake? That is what this book tries to do. The attempt has been made to steer away from abstract discussions and to deal with issues through looking at specific texts and their place in liturgical traditions. References are not given to academic works, though their influence is of course present.

Inevitably, given the experience of the author, there is considerable reference to the liturgy of the Church of Rome and to what goes on in Catholic congregations. However, for reference to scriptural selections most examples are found in the common lectionary produced by the Consultation on Common Texts for use in Canada and the United States of America. There is also frequent reference to uses and liturgies of churches other than the Catholic. It is hoped that the book will thereby serve the interests of communion between churches.

The work is divided into two parts. The first part, "Reading the Scriptures in the Liturgy," is addressed to how particular passages are heard when they are proclaimed in liturgical services, what questions they raise, and how they are interpreted. Due attention is paid to the context, the culture, and the prevailing questions of the communities who hear these readings. The second part, "Of Scriptures, Prayers, and Root Metaphors," is addressed to broader issues. Faith traditions that are informed by the scriptures show this influence in their rites and in their public prayer. Scriptural texts, images, and metaphors are worked into prayers and affect the choice of symbols and ritual actions. They in turn, however, are being constantly interpreted through this process. At different times, in their composition of liturgies or in their interpretation of them, churches allow one or another scriptural image to prevail, but this owes as much to cultural and public concerns as it does to exegesis. This raises questions about the exact nature of the relation of liturgy to its scriptural roots. The pertinence of this to liturgical renewal is taken into account in the second part of the book.

This book was already with the publisher when the Congregation for Divine Worship of the Roman Curia issued its new directives on translating liturgical texts.[1] There is nothing in the section on scriptural texts (nos. 34–45) that would alter the treatment of issues of interpretation and usage given here. Suffice to say that the instruction raises once again the need to keep a living tension and balance between fidelity to original biblical texts, respect for the traditional use in the Roman liturgy of the Vulgate version of the Bible, and a language that addresses persons in their contemporary world. Some of the precise directives of the instruction might be open to critical assessment, but that task is not germane to the subject of this book.

---

1. The Congregation for Divine Worship and the Discipline of the Sacraments, "Instruction: Liturgiam Authenticam," *Origins* 31, no. 2 (May 21, 2001): 17–32.

Part One

Reading the Scriptures
in the Liturgy

Chapter One

The Word of the Lord

O N A SUNDAY in the year 2000, according to the common lectionary reflecting the use of many Christian churches in Canada and the United States, the Gospel proclaimed at Mass was Mark's account of the healing of the woman who suffered from hemorrhages and of the raising of the daughter of the leader of the synagogue (Mark 5:21–43). In one congregation, inclined to charismatic prayer, the preacher told the people that if they had faith enough, they would see miraculous cures. In another, the homily noted that the point of the story was not really the cures, but to draw us to faith in Jesus Christ as the Lord of life and death. In yet a third place, the priest expounded on the legalities affecting the woman who would be considered unclean and unacceptable company because of her flow of blood; from this perspective, what Jesus did was to release her from the bondage of the Law and its regulations. Having read commentaries by Africans, I could well imagine a congregation in the Cameroun being invited to rely less on Western-style medicine and outside aid, and to turn more readily to their traditional healers and medications. In each of these celebrations, the proclamation was reverenced as the Word of the Lord and the Gospel of Christ.

In liturgical gatherings, scriptural texts are indeed proclaimed and presented as the Word of the Lord. This may seem to refer merely and clearly to what is in the book or to the passage that has been read. However, it is readily apparent that the text read has been taken out of its context in the Bible and put into a new context defined by the congregation and the celebration. Hence the question: Can we trust God's Word when it is put out of context any more than we trust quotations from persons given to us out of context? Or is the change of context a way of enlarging its force and its applicability?

3

For example, when the reading from Exodus 14 about the cross-ing of the Red Sea by the Israelites is proclaimed at the Paschal Vigil, the congregation hears nothing about how they first came to Egypt, nor about Moses' meeting with Yahweh in the burning bush, nor about the subsequent wandering through the desert for forty years. What meaning does the passage have when so treated?

In its liturgical setting, a text is now related to other texts, like-wise extricated from their written context. Thus at the Paschal Vigil the text already mentioned is related by a reading from Genesis with the story of creation, and it is also related by the night's ritual to the sacraments of initiation. The audience or congregation has been attuned to the commemoration of Christ's resurrection and to the celebration of baptism, and this colors how they hear the text and the meaning they find in its proclamation.

It is further apparent that the text has acquired meanings down through many centuries of Christian proclamation and Christian interpretation. The crossing of the Red Sea in the context of the Book of Exodus has nothing to do with baptism. The Christian community, however, related it to this sacrament from early times, in greater or lesser degree. During the centuries when baptism was celebrated at Easter, the relation was steadfast. When adult baptism was not a common practice, the water blessed on Holy Saturday was indeed intended to be kept in the font for infant baptisms, but it was also accredited a different kind of power in combating evil. People liked to keep "holy water" in their homes, and farmers took churns of blessed water from church on Holy Saturday to spread in their fields. This associated the waters, whether of creation, of the Red Sea, or of the baptismal pool, of which the scriptures spoke with a larger sense of the combat between the power of evil and the power of the good. When the stories were interpreted of baptism, sometimes they were read as a story of how God saves his people from sin and Satan. In other interpretations, the crossing of the sea was related more to the passage that the elect have to make from sin to grace. All such meanings given to it in the past lurk in the background whenever this text is now read.

It seems that the acclamation "Word of the Lord" affirms that the text has a meaning that comes from its liturgical context. It says that God addresses the congregation through the reading. But how? Within what context is this true? What meaning does it have? How does it get that meaning? In what sense can it be said that

God addresses the congregation through this Word and the particular meaning given to it here and now by its placement in the Paschal Vigil?

The Word of the Lord

The acclamation is familiar to all who frequent liturgies. The text is read from the lectionary of selected texts, and the reader concludes with the declaration, "The Word of the Lord." At times this is dramatized by holding the book aloft and presenting it to the assembled congregation. When it is the Gospel that is proclaimed, the book is first incensed.

Given this rather complex attention to the scriptures, we need to grasp more fully what it is to offer something as "the Word of God." The liturgical context of proclamation serves as ground for a good approach to hearing and interpreting the scriptures. It is often said that it is only within a faith community that the Word is properly passed on and understood. This is because it is by faith that the Word is received, transmitted, interpreted, and related to worship and to a life lived by faith in God and in Christ.

However, the ways in which scriptural texts are now received and pondered make this process rather more complex. The scriptural texts of any given day have perhaps first been discussed among groups of people, with somebody proffering a brief exegesis out of a scriptural commentary to start off the conversation. Those present then ask, "What does it mean to us?" and perhaps even argue about it. Somebody will remind the group of the exegesis, lest the discussion get out of hand. Somebody else will appeal to other texts. Some will want to see the text primarily in relation to feelings, others primarily in relation to ideas. Some may even impose some teaching of the Pope on it, thinking that meaning is always reducible to some easily intelligible proposition wherein $x = y+z$.

When these groups come together for the act of worship, they may hear a preacher speak who has given no attention to any commentary and who shows little interest in the discussions of Bible groups. This is noticed and members of the congregation readily write off what he is saying. In all of this, the congregation as it were is listening to a fragmented text, one torn into fragments by the way in which it is treated. The acclamation "the Word of the Lord" raises even more questions than those they already have, and the beautiful binding on the lectionary does not explain what is in it, though it may draw attention to it.

Of course there are ways of making do with this indecisive or even poor treatment of the Word proclaimed. If the responsorial psalm of the day is reasonably vibrant and allows for congregational participation, and the prayers of the faithful have brought up the things that bother and concern the people present, for the moment this gets over the dilemma of what the scripture says "today." Possibly, however, its meaning and significance have been simply deleted, and it never comes alive in the assembly.

What may it in fact mean to pay more attention to how a text addresses a congregation, or to how God addresses a congregation from a text and within the faith of the assembly? What the scripture may evoke can be exemplified by taking a particular text into consideration. Since the first draft of this work was taken up in the twenty-first week of the year 1999, we take the weekly Gospel lectionary of the Roman Catholic Church for that week, or at least the first three days of it.

Catholics who attended weekday Mass heard the woes of Jesus against the scribes and Pharisees found in Matthew's Gospel (Matthew 23), what indeed may be called his curses. In 1999, the feast of Saint Bartholomew intervened on the Tuesday and so interrupted the sequence with a reading for the feast of the apostle. Neither Bartholomew, however, nor any other saint could allow the community to escape the onslaught of these woes. They came back on the Wednesday, with maybe even a louder note of discordance. It is odd to hear Jesus cursing people, though indeed it shows how he belonged in quite a strong prophetic tradition and should not surprise us.

Those in positions of authority among the Jewish people at that time were castigated by Jesus, even cursed by him, for a preoccupation with ritual niceties which blinded them to God's presence among them and rendered them deaf to his teaching. So concerned were they about details of the Law that they could not find its essence or notice how it was coming to fulfillment. By chance, the Gospel text has a very adroit accompaniment in a reading from Paul's Letter to the Church of Thessalonika. The people of Thessalonika are disturbed over their own thoughts about the coming end of time, the advent of God's reign that will put an end to human history. Paul tells them not to be concerned about such things but to go on working. They should not indulge in reading signs or practice rituals which try to settle accounts before God does. He even tells them to look at his own example in persevering in his preaching, in working in serving others. Some of the people were missing the point of his Gospel teaching about the Christ because in their own ritual fasting they were trying to anticipate God's action and settle accounts according to their own perceptions and devices. This was another way to obscure the truth by a misguided ritual practice and preoccupations that prevented them from being open to God's judgments and God's action.

A striking thing about the Gospel text, thus complemented by Paul, is that it is a curse or condemnation. Those who felt uncomfortable about this in the week in question may have been reminded by a quite recent newspaper discussion about some words of Pope John Paul II on hell. Hell is not a place, he said. It is the state of those who have cut themselves off from God's Word, God's covenant, God's life. Clear enough, but the woes have a real ring of rejection. Anyway, to whom are they addressed "today" in the liturgy, or do they merely belong to a past, to the transition from Old to New Covenant so that we can leave Christ's curses securely in the past, laying them squarely on the shoulders of the scribes and Pharisees who picked on his words and deeds?

That may have been the comforting interpretation for Matthew's first readers. Matthew himself, however, goes beyond this. He does seem to want to make these words applicable to the leaders of the Church and to disciples in its community, inasmuch as they too are given to a legal nitpicking that blinds to the true sense of the words and actions of Jesus. Confining the meaning of the text to the dispute between Jesus and the scribes and Pharisees is certainly an interpretation that carried weight for centuries when the Jewish people were still called *perfidious*. The *tradition* may have sanctioned such an application, but it is time to break it, for it has done enough harm and sits unhappily with our memories of the Holocaust. It cannot be evoked without bad conscience in this broken world, whose story through the age of enlightenment and the modern world is impossible to tell without coming up against such horrendous and untellable events. And the memory always carries the question, "Where were the Christians?"

If one delves into the point of these verses in Matthew, one is struck by the parallels with the eight blessings of Matthew 5 and the curses spoken against the *goats* of the scene of kingly judgment in Matthew 25: "Depart from me, ye cursed." These are certainly not Jews, nor scribes, nor Pharisees. They are believers who did not feed the poor, comfort and nurse the sick, visit the prisoners. So how can the congregation in this parish church escape these curses? Where is the sting felt by readers and hearers in this predication of Jesus' curse?

The interfacing of the two scriptural texts for the day, and their resonance in the life of any church community or people, gives rise to thought about the ways in which believers may obscure the truth of the scriptures or conceal the manner of God's presence and action. It is as if each generation devised its own ritual and legal ways for escaping the deep implications of the Law and the Prophets, or the remembrance of Jesus Christ and his proclamation as Lord.

Hence an interpretation of these Gospel passages that passes from exegesis to the point of taking the meaning of the text into people's lives must ask, "In face of betrayal of religious traditions, do woes still ring out today?" It is not only a better knowledge of the scriptures that creates the disharmony felt in reading and hearing the text. It is the world to which the text is asked to apply, and the Church in which it is expected to ring true. The age on this cusp of the millennium is a broken one. The tradition of interpreting and preaching the Word of God is a broken one.

In this way, attending to the presence of one particular text in the lectionary opens up deeper considerations about the possibility of hearing the scriptures today. The broken character of the world for humankind in our age comes from appalling memories of violence and injustice. For the Western world it is the way in which social engineering and technology have managed existence that has come to the fore in all its deficiencies. For peoples of the African, Asian, and Latin American continents, their brokenness is apparent in the impoverishment of their traditions by conquest of their lands by foreigners and in the present tension between the retrieval of culture and the advent of forms of social, political, and economic enterprise, along with the means of global communication. For the peoples of eastern Europe and central Asia it is the breakdown first of monarchy and then of communism, and the mutual suspicion of followers of different religions. For every particular populace or congregation, there is a particular experience of betrayal and a particular situation of evil, even ecclesial evil, even one in which they are compromised, to curse or lament. The reading of the text from the Gospel of Matthew as a simple story of transition from Old to New Covenant does not hold, either in the face of exegesis, or in the face of Christian anti-Semitism and its compromise with fascism, or in the face of broken stories, or in the face of newly felt betrayals. Maybe the Church may see itself as the object of these curses for its impoverishment of peoples and their cultures through an overwrought reliance on Latin observances in its ritual and in its teaching. Or maybe some communities will find themselves challenged for neglecting questions of justice while being very particular about the requirements for sacramental celebration. As it has been asked, how can priests insist on imported wheaten bread for the Mass when the children have no millet?

The Church's Hearing of the Word

A number of observations can help us to place the meaning of the proclamation heard at the liturgy, "the Word of the Lord," or "the Gospel of the Lord." What is proclaimed is in fact a selection of texts made by the Church for the liturgy of the day. It is read and commented upon within a community of faith, its meaning already much determined by a long tradition. Since it is a community of faith, it is there to worship God, to receive gifts from God, to be nurtured, and to give praise. It is in its beliefs persuaded of the presence of God in its midst, through the love and power of Christ and through the Holy Spirit. It is there to move through the hearing of the scriptural texts to its prayers of thanksgiving, blessing, and intercession. All of this shapes the way in which the proclamation is received. What is heard is not simply a text from a book but a voice that expresses the faith of the Church and that is passed on in faith by the Church.

We do not know in much detail what the practices of the churches were in their early days. Before the New Testament canon took shape, there were readings from the Law, the Prophets, the Psalms, and wisdom literature. This was according to the words of the risen Lord recounted in the story of his encounter with the two disciples on the way to Emmaus, when he brought them to faith in the purpose of his suffering and death by opening up to them what was in the "Law and the Prophets." This was to interpret these scriptures in light of what the Church believed about Christ, in light of their belief in Christ. We do not know, however, how complete a reading the scriptures were given in the gatherings of the faithful, whether on Sundays or on weekdays. We also know that the selection of texts from the writings about Christ and from the letters of the Apostles for proclamation and comment in the assembly had an important part in determining what came to be known as the canon of the New Testament. Again, however, how much of these books were read we do not know. As read and commented upon, these texts were always related to the mystery of Christ and the people's participation in it, as they were also related to how they lived among themselves and in the societies of their day. This determination of meaning from faith and circumstance is of course already operative in the writings themselves as originally composed and presented to the churches of the New Testament era.

From a period when research allows us more insight into what was done, several things can be noted. In preparing hearers and catechumens for baptism and Eucharist, some effort seems to have been made to introduce them to quite a comprehensive knowledge of the scriptures. At the same time, the guiding rule for their interpretation was the Creed, that is, faith in Christ as lived in the community and handed on by the Church. For the assemblies of the faithful, there was a difference between weekday (noneucharistic) gatherings and Sunday congregations. The purpose of the former was largely to give praise to God through psalms, hymns, and prayers of intercession. Some instruction could be included and with this some exposition of the scriptures. Sunday gatherings were marked by a selection of texts rather than by an effort to read the entire Bible.

What is known most from early centuries is the selection of texts for the more important parts of the year. These are: the Paschal Cycle, with the preparation for Pasch and the fifty days leading to Pentecost; Christmas and Epiphany; the Advent season. While texts for these celebrations were not universally the same, it is clear that they were chosen and woven together in virtue of what was being celebrated. Elements of a continuous reading of particular books over the rest of the year are more in evidence, but even then there was a selection at work and a correlation of texts from different books within the same liturgy. All of this in effect marks the faith of the Church at work in what different communities chose for liturgical proclamation.

In his book *Scripture and Memory: The Ecumenical Hermeneutic of the Three-Year Lectionaries,*[1] Fritz West contrasts a Catholic principle with a Protestant principle in the compilation of liturgical lectionaries and in their interpretation. The Catholic principle is the one that harmonizes the choice of texts with the liturgical season and celebration. It interprets scripture primarily through liturgy. The Protestant principle, as West sees it, does the opposite. Its intent is to introduce a broad knowledge of the scriptures. Even when attaching specific texts to specific festivities is accepted in virtue of an ecclesial tradition, it is the scripture which serves as interpreter of the liturgy and not vice versa, and can even serve as a corrective of liturgical rite and prayer.

The three-year lectionary published by the Consultation on Common Texts[2] among members of several English-speaking churches seems to work on the basis of a compromise between the two principles. It respects the choice of particular texts for special seasons worked into the current Roman lectionary from ancient sources. On the other hand, it does its best to have a continuous reading of books and to work with the original scriptural books as far as possible. It refers to an early Church practice of having a continuous reading of books for the Sunday liturgy. This is true of course to a great extent outside the special Easter and Christmas cycles and outside other major feasts. This hardly makes it a general principle and the liturgical interpretation of scriptures may be revealed more in these special seasons than in practices of continuous readings.

In fact, in the light of liturgical tradition it would seem that the primary concern of liturgical usage of the scriptures is not to introduce congregations into a complete knowledge of the canonical scriptures. How much such knowledge served as a background to liturgy differed from age to age. In recent centuries, to know the whole Bible and to revere it as God's Word addressed to his people have become more important.

The principle of providing as much of the Bible as possible through liturgy is not therefore invalidated. Thomas Cranmer

---

1. Fritz West, *Scripture and Memory: The Ecumenical Hermeneutic of the Three-Year Lectionaries* (Collegeville, Minn.: Liturgical Press, 1997).

2. *The Revised Common Lectionary,* compiled by the Consultation on Common Texts (Nashville: Abingdon Press, 1992).

sought to give people this presentation of the entire scriptures through his structuring of morning and evening prayer. Protestant worship services have also been more devoted to the presentation and proclamation of the scriptures than Catholic services. Though the format of services in the Anglican and Reformation churches is changing today, as is that of Catholic services, it nonetheless remains a clear Catholic principle that the scriptures are to be heard and expounded within the context of worship and rite and in relation to the catechetical and doctrinal teaching of the Church. This affects not only matters of presentation but also those of translation. Latin translations were long the chief mode of transmission, and lectionary translations for today have to take the nuance given to texts through this transmission into account when asking whether to keep a text or to eliminate it.

Today, we will normally expect that congregations have fuller and more technical knowledge of the scriptures. This may be true because of courses in religion in schools and universities or because of seminars given at the parish level. It may also be true because of the reading done in basic Christian communities in different parts of the world or in small faith communities in others. This is an enrichment peculiar to our time and is not to be ignored in liturgical proclamation. However, the issue to be faced is the passage from this kind of knowledge to its hearing in the liturgical context and in conjunction with sacramental rites.

This then reminds us how much the use in worship is tied in to the faith and human concerns of people's lives. While a cursory acquaintance with tradition may not make this clear, further thought allows us to see how certain selections and interpretations did indeed relate to broader social and cultural realities. This can be developed more later on, but two instances of this may be cited.

First, the accentuation of the sacrificial motif in the Roman liturgy that was brought to bear on scriptural selections for the Pasch was validated from what it did for social context. In early days of the Roman Rite, this allowed Christians to locate the true sacrifice in Christ and the Eucharist, even as they refused participation in the sacrificial cults of the Roman Empire. In Carolingian and later times, the motif continued to serve the maintenance of social order and the distinctions that prevailed between orders in both the ecclesiastical and the civic world.

As a second example, we can take the Byzantine liturgies for

Easter, in their preparation and continuance through Bright Week.[3] In the emperor who resided at Constantinople the Church and its people saw a manifestation of the divine, and court ritual affected the development of the liturgy itself. However, far from being a veneration of the imperial court, what the liturgy did was to present the mystery of Christ's Pasch as his royal entrance into his city, thus adopting a social image to present the faith and how it influenced the Christian way of regarding worldly powers. That also affected the selection of texts, their relation to rites, and their interpretation.

This relation to current social, cultural, and economic issues is not foreign to liturgy and the meaning of the Word of God. Indeed, it is inherent to inserting texts into the living world and the living faith of a community. That such concern comes to bear on the hearing of the Word today follows, though in a more diverse world it is more difficult to work this out.

As situated within a context of worship, the hearing of the scriptures is prepared by prayer and rite and carries the people forward into sacramental action. It might be said that gathering in Christ's name, and the rites and prayers of gathering, dispose the people to hear the Word in faith and within the tradition of the Church's beliefs. It need also be said that the anticipation of what is to be done sacramentally also affects how the Word is heard.

As remarked above, often enough today standard or accustomed choices and interpretations are challenged or sit uneasily with members of the congregation. This is not destructive of the faith context but is inevitable as the life of the faith emerges from a different kind of background and relates to different issues. As a living tradition, organically developing within the life of a people, the Church's liturgy must naturally evolve in the way that it interprets scriptures and even in the selection of texts that are proclaimed.

Whatever the immediate purpose and practice in the choice of scriptural texts for services of worship, the hope and intent are to hear the Gospel of Christ, the Word of the Lord given to us in him. As one pair of authors deftly state, "authentic gospel... is talk of Christ which is (1) faithful to the remembered Jesus and (2) free response to the futurity of the risen Jesus."[4] Even if the typological

---

3. The name given to the week after Easter.
4. Eric W. Gritsch and Robert W. Jenson, *Lutheranism: The Theological Movement and Its Confessional Writings* (Philadelphia: Fortress, 1976), 11.

readings of earlier times, present also in the selection of liturgical readings, seem too far today from the original meaning of the scriptures, we share with this approach the purpose of hearing what is proclaimed through the prism of faith in Christ.

Within this vision and remembrance, the Church in its single congregations tries to understand better the letter of the text. It learns too from the readings of tradition. It is alert to the presence of God in the world and the active ways of a love that transcends self and self-interest. This of necessity means an encounter with suffering. There is the suffering of the death to self and to human autonomy, a suffering that is both personal and collective. There is most of all the suffering of those who are subjected to human injustice and cruelty. The God who is hidden on the cross in the suffering Christ is nonetheless revealed in the midst of this suffering. This is the promise, assurance, and hope which prepare the mind and heart to listen to the Word proclaimed and celebrated.

Open to the Word

To hear the Word as it is given to us, with all its variety of meanings, requires open minds and open hearts. Once we lay aside the illusion that the sense and impact of a text are fixed for all time, we can listen with greater attention, with the desire to receive what is being offered, and with the will to respond.

We know well from the way that literary works are passed on and enacted in public that their meaning cannot be exhausted and that it takes on fresh nuance in different settings. The plays of Shakespeare are put on stage in ways that give them a new twist. The same African American spirituals can be sung at weddings, at festivals, or at funerals, and respond to each of these occasions in suitable ways. Sometimes a curriculum enlarges the canon, and every piece in it then sounds differently.

To listen to the scriptures in their liturgical setting and in their life-setting, with the knowledge of what they have meant to tradition, is to listen with the readiness to be challenged. In effect, this is proper to the very nature of human existence, where the power of a word is incalculable. A term borrowed, knowingly or unknowingly, from the title of a book by the celebrated theologian Karl Rahner[5] is

---

5. Karl Rahner, *Hearers of the Word* (New York: Herder & Herder, 1969).

quite often used to describe human persons. They are called "hearers of the Word." The description latched on to the fact that it is inherent in human beings to grow and to attain growth in knowledge and wisdom through the hearing of a word, a word that is in a variety of ways addressed to persons, societies, and cultures. The call to be attentive to the voice of another person arises from the depth of one's being. This is transmitted, however, not only through spoken words, but also through written texts that are proposed to a people as a word that belongs to their heritage and that has been passed on to them from the past.

Beyond what may be an expected kind of discourse, there are words and stories that seem somehow intrusive. For North Americans of European origin, stories about the practice of marriage or the veneration of ancestors in indigenous societies or in African and Asian societies are strange. The word and its story do not belong evidently to the world around the people, and that word has not arisen from within their own culture or from their own past. If it is to be heard and received, it requires an attention and a response that stretch the hearers' capacity to grasp its meaning and to measure up to its call for empathy.

Just as there are widening disputes today over what should be included in the school or college canon of English and American literature, there are disputes over what ought to be included in the liturgical canon of scriptures. Texts with an anti-Semitic ring, or patriarchal texts, may be either shunned or listened to more critically. New texts can be introduced, as in the liturgies of marriage, baptism, or funerals.

Sometimes the new sounds intrusive. It is not that to which a community is accustomed. It is like the voice of a stranger. The intrusion of another voice may come from outside one's culture or may be something from the past which has hitherto been largely ignored, as when the Book of Ruth figures more prominently in the liturgical canon. This too is the Word of the Lord and asks for response. The more a person or a community allows this kind of word to affect their way of seeing things, the more one is opened to a horizon of reality that seems without limit. In very truth, the more we open mind and heart to stories that come from others, the more we may be aware of a call to hear a word from beyond, a word that precedes all beginnings to which we can give circumstance or date. All these strange words that we hear speak to us of a voice behind all voices, an address that cannot be precisely located or dated. The at times vague, and at times very intentional, use of the word "infinite" denotes the sense of being addressed from outside and beyond the world that we readily grasp. Such attunement to an address from the infinite and a call to the infinite capacity to hear and to respond is a necessary disposition of the soul in listening to the scriptures as God's Word.

While this openness to the infinite is a necessary disposition of spirit, it has to be accompanied by a willingness to be disturbed. Though highly alert to historical development and to the historical conditioning of the expression of truth, people today may feel that it is this openness to a sense of the transcendent which itself constitutes the hearing of God's Word. It is typical of people in our contemporary Western society, indeed even among Christians, to give great weight to getting to the person's internal self-awareness or consciousness of the self. When judged sincere and genuine, this may be taken as a guarantee of truth and arbiter of interpretation. True readiness to respond, however, tells us that this is not so. God and the call of the Gospel lie beyond human self-awareness and with their claims, maxims, and stories continue to disrupt our sense of identity and our command of the truth, asking for the willingness to give ourselves over to the Word that creates us and judges us and leads us whither we do not know and cannot anticipate.

Though this may not seem evident at first, in fact a contemporary mindfulness of the many meanings that may be given to one single text brings us to realize just how ungraspable, and at the same time grasping, the Word of God is. For many in the Church, a crisscrossing of interpretations seems confusing and threatening. In truth, however, it simply tells us that God's address out of its infinite generosity and call resounds differently in different persons, different communities, different times, and different places. A hearing of a text needs some preconditions in the hearer, to wit the cultivation of a certain way of looking on life. It is also affected by all the presuppositions about life that we carry to biblical interpretation. To think that we can hear any text with some kind of purity of original and intended meaning is an illusion. Nor does God expect this of his creatures. His Word is to resound within human lives, according to the patterns of historical and cultural conditioning and in relation to the events that have formed and form the world in which people live. Entering into such a world, that Word does challenge it, but it cannot challenge it unless it makes its way into it. If we are not to make our consciousness of self or our present understanding the final criterion of a fixed and final meaning, we need to see that within the human heart and within any community or society there is a dynamism that gives rise to constant inquiry, even while there is the acknowledgment that finally truth and meaning are not found by us but have to be given to us. It is not surely only the mind which is at work in such response but the heart is touched as well, with the readiness to allow affections and life-commitment to be played upon.

In virtue of this searching inquiry and readiness to be challenged, people are drawn to revisit texts already read or heard, and indeed to revisit standard or accepted interpretations in the light of how they have affected one's way, or a society's way, of living. This is what the poet Seamus Heaney calls the *canon of expectations,* according to which it is what lies under that may begin to speak.

Once this is said, what is called for is better attention to the conditions that determine human consciousness and self-identity, and hence the way one reads or hears the voice of another, or written texts that belong to a cultural or religious patrimony. The first thing to be taken into account is that, in fact, we are wounded and naked in face of words addressed to us. We cannot derive an understanding of the scriptures from an already existing, lucid self-awareness since the only way to act out of a true and faithful self is to listen to what texts or spoken words may say to us or what they reveal of us to ourselves, and to the testimonies given in the lives of those who live by these traditions. In approaching the Word of God, Christians do so in the hope of being able to recognize both their own sinfulness and their own power in the gift of God's Spirit. This light on the self is cast by the text written and proclaimed, even for those aware of the limits on their understanding and the tightening of their hearts. What is more fundamental and important is that readers and hearers are introduced to a world beyond their native ken in which the love and mercy of God dominate and prevail.

Conclusion

What is happening, then, is that the text is heard by people who cannot be satisfied by an explanation which either belongs totally to the beginnings of Christianity or is superficially moralistic. They are too conscious of changes in Christian dispensation and story and too conscious of the brokenness of the world in which we live at the turn of a millennium. They listen to the text, and discuss it, with certain questions and interests in mind. In fact, they are listening to a text which has taken on a rather complex life as it has found a hearing in Christian communities down through the ages.

But what does it mean to say that a text has a life?

Chapter Two

Life of a Text

T O ASCRIBE LIFE to a text is to say that it journeys across time within communities that read it and converse about it, so that it takes on a life in a way similar to that in which a person finds a life. Persons look back on their lives for meaning and project what is yet to come. They do this, not on their own, but in contact and interaction with other persons and communities. Texts such as the scriptures belong to and within communities. The reading of these texts has a past which shows the meaning given to them at different times. Read now they project a life that is yet to emerge through further interpretation, through encounter with other texts and with lived lives, and through action taken in accordance with what is found in them.

It is impossible to separate the transmission of texts across time and cultures from their relation to the spoken word. In the field of literature, those texts remain alive which are used in classrooms, spoken about in families, and quoted in political, cultural, and religious assemblies. A person may read a text or view a painting and find therein personal satisfaction, sustenance, and pleasure in so doing. The text or painting, however, becomes part of a living patrimony when discussed and interpreted in living conversation. The diffusion of texts through cheap reproduction, and even the reproduction of great works of art, make them more accessible and more likely to be assumed in one way or another into spoken forms of expression, rhetoric, and conversation. To some this may seem to debase such works, but it is their diffusion, however done, that gives them a place in a popular heritage.

As far as the texts of the Judeo-Christian scriptures are concerned, we can see by way of example how they have been and are an integral part of oral tradition. Even their written transmission is affected by their community usage. The lectionary used for sacraments and the prayer of the hours is a good touchstone. It is those parts of the Bible placed in these lectionaries that are best known, more often interpreted and commented upon, and thus related to Christian living. This goes side by side with the effort, as exemplified in the sixteenth century by Thomas Cranmer in his composition of the *Book of Common Prayer,* to bring the Word in its entirety to the people.

In this chapter, first to be considered is the transmission of texts within the setting of ritual. Second, the way in which the interpretation of such texts is influenced by the social and cultural setting of the liturgy will be considered. The study is done through the use of specific examples.

The Liturgical Transmission of Biblical Texts

Here we will consider a number of examples to illustrate how biblical texts are inserted into liturgies, with consequences for the meaning which is given to them by the rite and which they in turn give to it. The first example has to do with diverse placements of the one text. Two examples then show how a text is affected when it is woven into song. After that, it is seen how the meaning given to a text for doctrinal reasons has implications for its use in liturgy. The fourth example illustrates how an episode recounted in the scriptures becomes part of popular celebration, of poetry, and of doctrinal interpretation. Finally, we will see how different texts are related to one another within the matrix of a liturgical celebration.

A Migratory Text: Exodus 12

Liturgical settings give meaning to scriptural texts. They relate them to specific occasions and festivals. They interweave them with other texts. They locate them in the context of ritual and sacramental celebration.

To see how this works, we can take the example of the placement of the text Exodus 12 in the celebrations marking the annual commemoration of the death and resurrection of Christ. The text is about the sacrifice and eating of the Lamb at the time of the escape of the Israelite people from Egypt, under the leadership of Moses.

In the history of the liturgy, this text first occurs in the liturgy of Jerusalem for the Paschal Vigil, where it is part of the twelve-lesson vigil of readings. The verses included are Exod 12:1–24. This means that the passage concludes with the command to the people and their children to observe the rite of the Paschal Lamb in perpetuity. Along with Genesis 22 on the binding of Isaac, the text offers a biblical type of the sacrifice of Christ. Placed within the vigil and its sacraments, it relates its meaning to the mystery of the Lord's death and resurrection which the Church commemorates on this night. Concluding with the command to keep ritual memorial, it establishes continuity between the history of Israel, the mystery of Christ, and the Christian memorial of his Passover.

It has been noted by scholars that though the episcopal Paschal liturgy of the Church of Rome shows some influence of the Jerusalem liturgy upon it, this particular text was never used at the vigil there. The reason offered is that the Church of Rome was more inclined to affirm discontinuity between the old dispensation and the new. Early versions of the blessing and praise of the Paschal Candle make no mention of the Lamb. At a later time, in commemorating the events of this night the hymn does mention the Lamb which was killed and whose redemptive blood marked the doorposts of the Israelites. There are also quite early prefaces to the eucharistic prayer which look to the Lamb as a figure of Christ, along with the offerings of Abel, Abraham, and Melchisedech. While these later three occur in the fixed part of the canon, mention of the Lamb does not. In any case, to present the Lamb as a figure or type of Christ, because of the power of its blood, does not make mention of the memorial command and establishes only a continuity of type, not one of ritual.

When the commemoration of the Paschal Mystery was extended backwards to include Good Friday, the Roman Rite included Exodus 12 in the readings for that day, preceding the reading of the Passion according to John. The verses chosen are Exod 12:1–11, concluding with the phrase: "This is the Phase, that is the passage of the Lord." The selection does not proceed as far as the ritual memorial command to observe this meal in commemoration of the Lord's action for his people. The psalm to be sung following the reading is Psalm 139 (140), which is the prayer of a just man persecuted by his enemies and refers more directly to the suffering and death of Christ than to the story of the Lamb.

Set before the reading of the Passion, this is indeed what is highlighted. In Exodus 12, the verse that stands out is the one that reads: "The whole multitude of the children of Israel shall immolate it at evening." The narrative of the Passion in the Gospel of John several times mentions that particular episodes in the Passion of Christ occur in fulfillment of the scriptures. This includes the piercing of the side of Christ with the soldier's lance, which was done so as to fulfill the scripture which says, "You shall not break any of its bones." This is a conflation of Zech 12:10, about the piercing of the side of one persecuted, and Exod 12:46 + Num 9:12, which prescribe that the lamb chosen for the Paschal Meal should not have a broken bone. The Gospel is already quite free in the way in which it quotes scripture texts, and the Christian liturgy follows suit.

In brief, it is clear that any of the references to the Paschal Lamb of the Jews in the Papal Roman liturgy is by way of seeing in it a figure or type of Christ's sacrifice. There is no desire to establish any kind of ritual continuity between Old Law and New, whether it be in reference to the vigil, as at Jerusalem, or specifically to the Christian Eucharist. However, in the revised liturgy of the Triduum of 1951 and onwards, Exod 12:1–8, 11–14, is assigned to Holy Thursday's evening liturgy of the Lord's Supper.[1] This selection concludes with the command to keep the memorial feast. The passage is linked in this liturgy with the reading from 1 Cor 11:23–26 about the institution of the Lord's Supper or Eucharist, which also finishes with a memorial command. From this concatenation, it is quite clear that the Eucharist, commemoration of the Lord's death and blood covenant, is being interpreted in light of the Jewish Paschal memorial. The psalm to be sung after the reading of Exodus is Psalm 116, which is a song of thanksgiving for the good that God has done to his people. It includes reference to the cup of salvation and to a sacrifice of thanksgiving in fulfillment of vows made. The refrain is taken from Paul, "Our blessing-cup is a communion with the blood of Christ." This also serves to draw out specific aspects of the commemorative ritual of the Eucharist.

In the 1979 *Book of Common Prayer* for the Episcopal Church in the United States, Exodus 12 is included for Holy Thursday and the psalm chosen to go with it is Psalm 78. This is a lengthy psalm about the importance of keeping memory of God's salvific actions, in obedience to his memorial commands. The verses chosen for the liturgy, however, verses 14–20, 23–25, focus on the types of the Eucharist in the Exodus story, such as the water that flowed from

---

1. This is also the place where it is now found in the Anglican liturgy in England and in the Episcopal liturgy in the United States.

the rock and the manna given in the desert. The Lutheran liturgical revision, on the other hand, places Exod 12:1–14 *or* 1–24 among the readings for the vigil, where it belonged in the early Jerusalem tradition.

These references to liturgies reveal the ritual migrations of the text from Exodus 12, with implications for the meanings given to it within celebration. In Jerusalem (and when used now in some churches), it referred to the Paschal Vigil and suggested a continuity from Jewish ritual and salvation history to the death of Christ and the Christian commemoration of it. In the Roman liturgy this was not included in the Vigil, but when the text was assigned to Good Friday the purpose was to give a typological reading of Christ's death. This was also in keeping with the mentions made of the Lamb in the vigil liturgy, whether in the praise of the Paschal Candle or in the eucharistic preface. In the more recent extension of the Triduum celebration, the Roman, Episcopal, and Anglican Rites employ the text to give Paschal significance to the eucharistic commemoration of the Lord's death and resurrection and to heighten the sense of the memorial command of the Lord.

Weaving Texts into Liturgical Song

Before discussing the transmission of any scriptural texts, it is helpful to go outside them and look at a living example of how oral transmission as such works. It is of course ironic that we can do this because of what has been put into writing, but that itself shows how cultural and social transmission often works. It still serves to show how a text heard may be both respected and transformed when brought into a new context. It is pertinent to a grasp of ritual tradition since even when written texts are read they are brought in ritual into the practices and traditions of orality.

Before looking at a couple of texts as used in liturgical song, a look at a poem within a nonbiblical oral tradition illustrates the process at work.

A Poem of the Basotho People

The example taken is that of how a praise song is used among the people of Lesotho in southern Africa.[2] It shows how this song

---

2. I found this poem when I was on a visit to the Republic of South Africa in 1999 but cannot now locate its provenance.

is accommodated to two quite different situations. By history, the Basotho are a pastoral and warrior people. Different clans often warred among themselves for domination of territory and possession of flocks. Warriors were held in high esteem, their prowess, feats, and qualities praised. At the same time, war wrought havoc and extinguished many a fighter in the bloom of manhood. Thus along with respect for war, there went a great desire for peace. The song transcribed below combines praise of warrior feats, lament for the dead, and a prayer for peace.

In more recent times, the people of Lesotho have been subjugated to an industrial economy which places them under the yoke of their larger neighbor, the Republic of South Africa. The young men no longer contend over pastures and herds but go down from the mountains into the worker camps of South Africa. There it is work in the mines and the risks of disease and violence that carry off the country's men folk. As given in the second column of Table 2.1 (both songs are presented as transcribed by a researcher), the old warrior song has been adapted to the remembrance and praise of those caught in the life of the mines and the camps. What appears to be a life of drudgery and pain is exalted because it has become the way in which the young may serve their families at home and contribute to the social welfare of their people. On the other hand, the lament over the dead and the plea for survival and liberation are as urgent as were those for the men caught up in war.

Certain similarities between the two songs reveal the convergence of interest and concern, as well as the respect for a tradition and its values, granted that the setting for the song is so different in each of the two cases. A respect for the past and a sense of the heroic carry over across time. A dominant metaphor in both renderings is that of the vulture, the carrion bird, who hovers over the site of conflict, with its looming threat and premonition of death. In both cases too, it is clear that while the protagonists are praised for what they have given, in strife and in death, to their people, the plea of the poem is for peace and an end to death. The more recent poem, building on the warrior tradition, does honor to the migrant mine-workers precisely by associating them with their warrior ancestors. The use of this form and tradition of praise song is a recognition that what they suffer, even death itself, in the mines and in the camps is a heroic action undertaken for the sake of their own people. In this sense, the horizon or perspective of the tradition remains the same

Table 2.1

Warrior Praise Song	Worker-Camp *Sefela*
Birds that are white, carrion lovers; The vultures spoke in Sesotho from the space of heaven, They spoke and thanked the Ditjotjela Regiment; And afterwards they begged for peace from the Lion of the Dinare Regiment Saying: "Sewelha-warrior, let them be, we beg you!" The birds cried "Hold!" to the Son-of-the-King, You have slaughtered for us amply, Ambusher-son-of-Mokhachane! Heed us! Many are the heads of men that lie upon the ground!	It's raining at Mamphororong: Death, cease hovering over me, My heart is tormented: let me sleep. Vulture of the oxen, black-winged, White-crested black one of the joiners, Fighters without hope. Men, Cattle! I salute you, I, Brother of Makhoathi!

in both songs: suffering and death for one's people have been made both necessary and heroic. However, the people yearn for an end to the death and the violence involved and look to an era of life and of peace yet to come.[3] In short, remembrance of the past builds a future for the present, and traditional values are given a living expression through forms of speech and song inherited from bygone days.

Turning from this cultural example to the use of Judeo-Christian scriptures in song, we will take two examples. These are the use of some verses from the Book of Lamentations and from Psalm 8, respectively.

Liturgical Use of Lamentations 1:12

This first example concerns a single verse, taken from the Book of Lamentations and used in different Christian settings of worship where lament is pertinent. The first column of Table 2.2 on the following page gives a critical English rendering of the Hebrew original; the second column gives an English rendering of the version found in the Latin Vulgate, since it was in the latter form that it

---

3. One would also need to consider the body movement, the ritual action, and the vocal tone, which would have been integral to both renderings and constitutive of the oral transmission/tradition. While the gum-boot dance of workers in South African mines has of late become an interesting theatrical diversion for American and European audiences, for those who dance it is an association with a much longer ritual tradition and an expression of cultural identity "in a strange place." Watching it on stage is somewhat like viewing a medieval altar piece in an art gallery.

Table 2.2

English, from the Original Hebrew	Latin Vulgate Version, with an English Translation	Use of the Verse in Office of Tenebrae, Holy Saturday, Second Nocturn, as a Liturgical Refrain to a Reading from Augustine[4]	Use in Procession to the Tomb with Cross and Sacrament on Good Friday, and Then within the Passion Play
"Is it nothing to you, all you who pass by? Look and see if there is any sorrow like my sorrow [which was brought upon me, which the Lord inflicted on the day of his fierce anger]." =The lament of Jerusalem over her destruction, as punishment by the Lord.	"O vos omnes, qui transitis per viam, attendite, et videte si est dolor sicut dolor meus." [O all you who pass along the way, pay attention, and see if there is sorrow like my sorrow.]	"O vos omnes, qui transitis per viam, attendite, et videte si est dolor sicut dolor meus." [O all you who pass along the way, pay attention, and see if there is sorrow like my sorrow.] =Lament placed in the mouth of Christ.	=Lament (as given in preceding column) placed in the mouth of Mary.

was incorporated into worship. The third and fourth columns give examples of how the text was used in contexts of Christian celebration, the one more formally liturgical, the other that of popular piety as it was in some ways accommodated by the clergy into the marking of the days of the Holy Triduum of our Lord's Passion and death.

The verse in its original setting is placed in the mouth of the city of Jerusalem, as she laments over the destruction and suffering she has endured from her invaders. It is voiced as a lament over a suffering brought on by sin, as an action of divine wrath and injustice visited on the city on account of the sin of its inhabitants. When the verse is put into the Roman Office of Tenebrae on Holy Saturday, it is used as a refrain to readings from Augustine about the Passion of Christ. These readings, in the Second Nocturn, follow readings from the Book of Lamentations that constitute the First Nocturn of the Office. The meaning given to the verse, and by implication to the readings from the Book, is determined from the context as a lament

---

4. Augustine, *St. Augustine on the Psalms,* trans. Scholastica Hebgin and Felicitas Corrigan (Westminster, Md.: Newman Press, 1960), on Ps 63:7.

over the sufferings both of Christ and of sinners, the former, however, being undertaken for the sake of the latter. The single verse of
the refrain is placed in the mouth of Christ, who asks others to join
him in lamenting over the suffering which he endures on account
of sin, which by reason of divine justice brings on the punishment
of suffering.

In the latter Middle Ages, the verse was incorporated into a Good
Friday procession to the tomb of Christ. This was a popular procession organized by confraternities that followed the day's official
liturgy. It was also at the time used in the Passion play. The verse is
placed in the mouth of Jesus' mother, Mary, who calls on the other
holy women and on all who pass by to lament with her over her
dead Son. It takes on a more poignant quality as the lament of a
mother over her Son. Though it is still a plea for compassion with
Christ and a plea for conversion from sin, it now has the social and
cultural force of a mother's lament.

Despite these different settings and renderings, the orientation
and concern of the text remain the same in the course of its transmission from written source to diverse oral renderings. It is always
addressed to a suffering inflicted and endured on account of sin, and
a suffering attributed to God's justice. But through its liturgical usage, it is affirmed that this suffering, due sinful humanity, has been
taken on by Christ, who by his cross appeases the divine justice by
God's own plan. In the last instance here given, through the person
of Mary all are called upon to lament over Christ's suffering, and
in this to lament over sin itself.

It is helpful to remember that the social, religious, and cultural
context of the time of the development of Tenebrae and then of the
Good Friday procession interpreted the death of Jesus in terms of
the prevailing view of justice. A right order could be established
only by retribution for offenses committed. The death of Jesus on
behalf of sinners was thus seen as an act of retribution to the God
who was offended. However, the divine excess in giving God's own
Son for this purpose eats into prevailing notions of justice and punishment, which are tempered by mercy and love. As these contexts
are looked at today as constituent parts of tradition, the metaphor
of retributive justice may not be very welcome. How the death of
Jesus for sinners may be seen, however, and how this both expresses
love and affects justice remain an issue. What might be done with
lament in liturgical celebration is also a question.

Psalm 8:4b–5

The next example of this kind of liturgical use of a scriptural text
is taken from the integration of a psalm, Psalm 8, which has played
a part in the development of christological themes in the Church's
tradition. What makes it pertinent today is the effort to give an
English translation of the original Hebrew words that is inclusive
rather than exclusively masculine. What is given in Table 2.3 is a
chart comparing the original Hebrew, the use of this psalm in the
Letter to the Hebrews, and its subsequent use in Christian liturgy.
Finally, there is the English translation of the psalm offered by the
International Committee on English in the Liturgy (ICEL).

Table 2.3

From Hebrew Original	Hebrews 2:6–8	Vulgate, for Liturgical Use	ICEL
What is Man that thou are mindful of him, and the Son of Man that thou didst care for Him?	What is Man that thou are mindful of him, and the Son of Man that thou carest for him?	What is Man that thou are mindful of him, or the Son of Man that thou hast visited him?	What is humankind that you remember them, the human race that you care for them?
Yet thou hast made him little less than God, and dost crown him with glory and honor. Thou didst give him dominion over the works of thy hands; thou hast put all things under his feet.	Thou didst make him for a little while lower than the angels, thou hast crowned him with glory and honor, putting everything in subjection under his feet.	Thou didst make him for a little while less than the angels, thou didst crown him with glory and honor; thou didst set him over the works of your hands. Thou didst put all things under his feet.	You treat them like gods, dressing them in glory and splendor. You gave them charge of the earth, laying all at their feet.

What we have in this example is a christological use of an Old
Testament psalmodic text. This meaning is first given to the text in
the Letter to the Hebrews. It occurs in two places in the ancient
and current Latin liturgy. The first usage is on Tuesday of the first
week of ordinary time, where the psalm is used as a response to
Hebrews 2. The second use is on Saturday of the twenty-eighth
week of the year, where it is used as a response to Eph 1:15–23,
where it also is given a manifestly christological meaning.

The text has generated controversy in recent years because of the problems raised for the translation of both the psalm and the Letter to the Hebrews by the International Commission on English in the Liturgy. The commission has offered a translation which is faithful to the original Hebrew. From one point of view this is quite correct, but in suggesting this for use in the liturgy, the commission has set aside the christological use of the psalm already introduced by Hebrews and then pursued in the Roman tradition by use of the Latin of the Vulgate edition of the Bible.

Hebrews

That there was such an early oral orientation to use of the psalm is testified by Phil 3:21, Eph 1:22, and 1 Cor 15:25. Hebrews applies this psalm to Christ, to make the point that it is to him that all things are subjected. But the letter substitutes "angels" for "God" and gives these verses an interpretation that refers to the humiliation of Jesus in the flesh and then to the exaltation by which all things are made subject to his dominion. This meaning is followed in patristic commentaries[5] and is adopted in the Roman liturgy which uses the Latin Vulgate. The ICEL has tried to return to the original sense of the psalm, in inclusive gender language, but as so translated it is no longer suitable to its established christological usage within the celebration of the liturgy. Obviously, at this stage of the textual and oral transmission a whole set of issues and interests have arisen which are quite different from the redemptive interpretation of many of the psalms that served to generate Christian piety in prayer. Hence we have a good example of how changing perspectives and interests may give rise to a different way of using a biblical text in oral execution, while also raising problems for the respect of past liturgical traditions.

The Supper Narrative in Liturgical Traditions

At this point we turn to an example that shows how an interpretation of a text affected its placement in the liturgy of the Eucharist. We can see how Martin Luther's understanding of the Latin word *testamentum* worked its way into the place which he gave to the Supper account found in 1 Corinthians 11, allying this with his

---

5. Ibid., on Psalm 8.

criticism of what he saw as the Latin liturgy's neglect of the proclamation of this text. It is of course from written texts that we know
Luther's mind, and from them we can trace what Luther thought of
the oral setting of the Supper Narrative in the liturgy and how this
relates to the ritual practice of the Mass.

The background is found in his use of the eighth and ninth chapters of the Letter to the Hebrews in his work "Treatise on the New
Testament, That Is, the Holy Mass."[6] First, it is to be noted that
Luther was reading the scriptural texts in their Latin version, so
that where in contemporary translations we read "covenant" he
read *testamentum,* or "testament." Hence he could speak of the
new and lasting testament which Jesus left to the Church through
the apostles in his Supper command. This testament was the promise of the forgiveness of sins and the donation of his body and blood
to seal this promise, as this is proclaimed in the words of the Supper:
this is my blood poured out for you and for many *for the forgiveness of sins.* As far as Luther is concerned, this proclamation and
sacramental gift ought to be at the center of the liturgy of the Mass.
Hence he cut out the words of the Roman canon that spoke of sacrifice and had the minister proclaim aloud the Supper Narrative and
proceed at once to the distribution of communion.

Luther's interpretation of the words of Jesus at the Supper, based
on his reading of the Letter to the Hebrews, fitted well with his
criticism of the Latin Mass and allowed him to insert this reading into the performance of the liturgy. Thus into the renewal of
the liturgy he inserted a living interpretation of the New Testament
text about the Supper. Thereby he also offered an interpretation of
the liturgical action which takes place regularly in the life of the
community.

This cannot be grasped fully unless we take notice of the context, religious and cultural, into which Luther's liturgical reform
fitted. The urgency of Luther's action followed on his critique of
a practice and a spirituality inherent in the Roman celebration of
the Mass which he saw as the embodiment of works righteousness.
This meant for Luther a reliance on the performance of ritual and
good works which took away from the total reliance of Christian
and Church on Jesus Christ and on the forgiveness of sins offered

---

6. "Treatise on the New Testament, That Is, the Holy Mass," in *Luther's Works*
(Philadelphia: Fortress, 1955–), 35:94ff.

in him, and in him alone. The audience was the broad cultural and religious world of the time and more proximately those who lived in the anxiety of their sinfulness because of their inability to meet the standards of behavior and action imposed by the laws of works righteousness. Luther aimed certainly at a renewal of faith. This renewal was made possible within the oral setting of proclamation in word and ritual, or word and sacrament. In brief, in this example of the use of a scriptural text we see an audience, an interrelation of texts, an interest and concern with a world of piety and practice, and an intention to put this Gospel into the setting of oral and sacramental converse.

Mary at the Foot of the Cross

At this point we can look at the transmission of a text which allies Gospel, liturgical piety, and doctrinal interpretation. In two separate tables, first we parallel passages from three Gospel accounts of the scene of the crucifixion to point up their contrast, related to the way in which this story was passed on in different communities (see Table 2.4 on the following page). Then we run the "Stabat Mater," texts from the Byzantine liturgy, and the poem "Crucifixion" parallel to each other (see Table 2.5). Some words of Pope John Paul II are added to show what is said doctrinally about Mary's role, something that has to be seen against the background of scripture and devotional or liturgical piety.

This example has to do with Mary's part in the Passion narrative of her Son, Jesus Christ. First, a comparison between Gospels shows how the transition is made from describing the presence of some of the disciples and women looking on "at a distance" to the presence only of women who are named but do not include Mary, to the presence of Mary, Mary of Magdala, and the disciple whom Jesus loved at the foot of the cross, addressed there by Jesus before he gives up the spirit. Then we see how in the thirteenth-century hymn of Jacopone da Todi this scene is transposed into an ardent description of Mary's suffering, into an active part by Mary in transmitting the benefits of her Son's redemption, and into her exemplarity as a follower on the way of the cross. This hymn was used in popular devotion, especially on Good Friday, and was also incorporated into a liturgical feast in honor of the Seven Dolours (or Sorrows) of Mary. Alongside this, we see how the scene at the foot of the cross was incorporated in the Byzantine liturgy's Good Friday celebration.

Table 2.4

Mark	Luke	John
When the sixth hour came there was darkness over the whole land until the ninth hour. And at the ninth hour Jesus cried out in a loud voice: "Eloi, Eloi, lama sabachtani?" which means, "My God, My God, why have you forsaken me?"...But Jesus gave a loud cry and breathed his last. And the veil of the Sanctuary was torn in two from top to bottom...There were some women watching from a distance. Among them were Mary of Magdala, Mary who was the mother of James the younger and Joset, and Salome.	It was now about the sixth hour and the sun's light failed, so that darkness came over the whole land until the ninth hour. The veil of the Sanctuary was torn right down the middle. Jesus cried out in a loud voice saying, "Father, into your hands I commend my spirit." With these words he breathed his last...All his friends stood at a distance; so also did the women who had accompanied him from Galilee and saw all this happen.	Near the cross of Jesus stood his mother and his mother's sister, Mary the wife of Clopas, and Mary of Magdala. Seeing his mother and the disciple whom he loved standing near her, Jesus said to his mother, "Woman, this is your Son." Then to the disciple, he said, "This is your mother." And from that hour the disciple took her into his home. After this, when Jesus knew that all was now finished, he said in order to fulfill the scriptures, "I am thirsty."...Then he bowed his head and gave up his spirit.

The twentieth-century poem by the Russian poet Anna Akhmatova takes the same scene as a backdrop and a metaphor for a literary piece that springs from a mother's sorrow over the loss of her son during the troubled Bolshevik era in Russia. The woman represented had stood many long hours under Stalin's regime outside the prison where her son was held captive. Now Mary's sorrow, as it were, has become unspeakable, something on which nobody can look, even as Jesus tells her not to weep for him when he goes abandoned by the Father to the grave.

Finally, by way of contrast we can consider some words of Pope John Paul II in a doctrinal context where he gives a theological interpretation to the scene and to Mary's part in it:

The mystery of the Incarnation and Redemption is described as a total self-emptying (Phil 2:5–8) which leads Christ to experience fully the human condition and to accept totally the Father's plan. This is an emptying of self which is permeated by love and expresses love. The mission follows this same path and leads to the foot of the cross...Mary is the

Table 2.5

Jacopone da Todi[7] (incomplete text)	Byzantine Liturgy, Holy Friday Matins, Antiphon XV to Proclamation of Passion[8]	Anna Akhmatova "Crucifixion"[9] (1940–1943)
Stabat mater dolorosa iuxta crucem lacrimosa, dum pendebat filius.	When she who conceived Thee, O Christ, Saw thee hanging on the cross, she cried out: What strange mystery do I behold, O my Son? O giver of life, how dost Thou die, Nailed on the wood in the flesh?	"Do not weep for me, Mother, When I am in my grave" A choir of angels glorified the hour, the vault of heaven was dissolved in fire. "Father, why hast thou forsaken me? Mother, I beg you, do not weep for me..."
Cuius animam gementem, contristatam et dolentem, pertransivit gladius.		
Pro peccatis suae gentis vidit Iesum in tormentis, et flagellis subditum.		
Vidit suum dulcem natum moriendo desolatum, dum emisit spiritum.	**Holy Friday Canon, Ikos**	Mary Magdalene beat her breasts and sobbed, his dear disciple, stone-faced, stared. His mother stood apart. No other looked into her secret eyes. Nobody dared.
Iuxta crucem tecum stare, et me tibi sociare in planctu desidero.	Beholding her own lamb led to the slaughter, Mary followed with the other women, in distress and crying out: "Where goest Thou, my child? Why does Thou run so swift a course? Surely, there is not another wedding in Cana to which Thou now dost hasten to change water into wine? Shall I come with Thee, my child, or shall I wait for Thee? Give me a word, O Thou who art the Word. Do not pass me by in silence, O Thou who didst keep me pure, for Thou art my Son and my God."	
Fac ut portem Christi mortem, passionis fac consortem, et plagas recolere.		

model of that maternal love which should inspire all who cooperate in the Church's apostolic mission for the rebirth

---

7. Sequence for the Feast of the Seven Dolours of Mary, 15 September, in *Missale Romanum* (New York: Benziger Brothers, Editio Iuxta Typicam, 1961).

8. *Holy Friday Matins with the Passion Gospels and Royal Hours,* prepared by John Erickson and David Anderson, 2d ed. (New York: Department of Religious Education of the Orthodox Church of America, 1980), 73.

9. "Requiem—10," in *Poems of Akhmatova,* selected and trans. Stanley Kunitz with Max Hayward (Toronto: Little, Brown and Company, 1973), 113.

of humanity...Mary's mediation is totally oriented toward
Christ and tends to the revelation of his salvific power...[10]

In the transmission of these texts related to Mary's place at the
foot of the cross, what we see on the one hand is the interpretative
character of the Gospel narratives which give quite different accounts of the crucifixion scene, of the words spoken by Jesus on the
cross, and of the presence of other persons. Each makes some point
for the reader about this scene and its meaning. Then the hymn "Stabat Mater" shows how medieval Western piety and poetry played
on this scene, augmenting the role of Mary in Christ's death and her
role in salvation. The texts from the Good Friday Byzantine liturgy
also develop Mary's role in the crucifixion of her Son. Akhmatova,
though Russian, had lived in Paris and was familiar with both traditions. These two sung texts therefore show how the Gospel story
was remembered and provides the background that makes both the
poem of Akhmatova and the doctrine of Pope John Paul II possible,
even though they turn to it in quite different senses.

Readings at the Paschal Vigil

We can now pass to an examination of the conjunction of different
texts, or of the play between texts, in the liturgy. A clear example
of this is found in the celebration of the Paschal Vigil, as celebrated
in Jerusalem and in the early liturgy of the Roman Church. It is
not that such intertextuality is taken without question. The point
for the moment is to see how connecting certain texts leads to a
particular interpretation.

While there were obviously other texts proclaimed at the vigil,
what will be considered here is the relation to the Passion and resurrection narratives of Exodus 12 on the Paschal Lamb, and of
Genesis 22 on the binding or sacrifice of Isaac. It can also be seen
how these texts are creatively related within the ritual to the initiation of neophytes into the community of the Church which partakes
as one in the eucharistic meal of the true Paschal Lamb, who is Jesus
Christ, crucified and risen. Clearly, it is in a living and sacramental
relation of faith and love to the one living Christ that the scriptural
texts are proclaimed and interpreted.

---

10. Pope John Paul II, encyclical letter *Redemptionis Donum* (1984).

In the proclamation of the Word, the imagery of redemption and sacrifice found in the two first narratives is assumed into a proclamation of the saving death and resurrection of Christ. This saving action is given a meaning through the use of the stories of the Lamb and of Isaac as types of Christ. Both episodes portray the action of sacrifice, but this is not reducible simply to an act of offering. In the case of the Paschal Lamb, the saving power of its blood and the partaking of its flesh in a common meal, in preparation for the journey of the exodus from slavery to freedom, are to the fore. In the story of Isaac, often referred to in Jewish lore as the binding of Isaac, both Abraham's willingness to sacrifice his son for the sake of God's covenant with his people, and what had come to be seen as Isaac's willingness to give up his own life, are pertinent to the imagery of Christ's death. So also is the intervention of God to prevent the death. When this text plays within a Christian vision of redemption, God's own willingness to hand over his Son to death, and the Son's willingness to accept death, are proclaimed and celebrated. So also is the divine intervention to prevent the power of death taking over. Though bound for sacrifice, Isaac/Jesus is given life and becomes the first born of many. In him, the promises made by God to Abraham and his descendants, to Moses and the people held in the bondage of Egypt, are fulfilled. On this particular night of the Pasch, they are passed on to those who are saved through the exodus of baptism, and anointed in the life of the Spirit, and now partake in the Eucharist of the true Paschal Lamb, who is Jesus Christ.

Summary Conclusion

The perusal of these examples opens the way to further considerations on the life of a text, such as it is acquired through the process of oral and ritual transmission, which then turns up in written form. The first thing to be noted is how a written text is, by the very fact of being set in writing, distanced from its original context and purpose. These are not negated, but a written text has a quality that makes it stand somewhat apart from its original composition so that it is available for reading and declamation in a variety of different settings and contexts, and even to be put to use for diverse, if not unconnected, purposes. That this may indeed on occasion spell betrayal of the text has to be taken into account, but this possibility is not now the immediate focus of comment.

Any written text in its production belongs to a given cultural—and religious, where this is pertinent—context. It has an author of whom something is known, and this author has a given audience in mind. On production, it fits into its immediate world, giving insight into it, commenting upon it, affirming it, or questioning it. There is a living community, a set of discussions, a place and a time, a writer with something to say, behind every written text. Of its nature, however, whatever its immediate purpose and reception, the writing on the pad or in the book (or presently on the computer disk) looks beyond the immediate. It has a life-line that survives the time of its presentation to the public. We tend of course to speak of texts that are read well after the death of their author and their epoch as classics, but in a way all written texts aim at a longer life than a first printing. They have something to say that endures beyond the immediate, that speaks of meanings or values or events that can carry over into another time and another cultural milieu. They invite this insertion, and so they invite an interpretation that is not confined to their moment of appearance but takes into account this other world and age. In short, to produce a text, even for a very clear original purpose, is to project its world, its horizon, its reference to events, its meanings, its linguistic skills, into contexts without number, wherein it will engage a different set of issues and questions.

The second aspect of the life of a text to be addressed is what happens when in fact it is read, and more specifically engaged in oral converse, in another context. It is offered to a new audience with its concerns and questions, it is brought into the oral (and ritual) interaction of persons, it is placed in relation to a number of other texts and rites, and it is taken up within the horizon of the interests and concerns of a different community and social environment.

Transmission and Social Setting

It is now time to see how scriptural texts, already given a place in the life of the Church through their liturgical placement, may still be variously understood within a diversity of cultural and social settings. This point will be illustrated by continuing with the texts first used in the Paschal Vigil and later, in a liturgically changed way, within the Triduum of the Roman liturgy.[11]

---

11. The main point to be noted here is that in the development of the Roman Triduum from Thursday to Saturday of Holy Week, Exodus 12 was no longer read

Earlier Settings

In the early Jerusalem and Roman liturgy, the audience was the congregation gathered to celebrate the Pasch and to receive its neophytes. The oral context is that of the night vigil and the celebration of the sacraments of initiation into Christ and the Church, which is gathered at the table of the Paschal Lamb. Taking their sacrificial imagery as a touchstone, we shall see how the understanding of these texts fits into a variety of settings and may vary according to these settings.

In the situation of the early Christian Church before the age of Constantine, we can see how the proclamation of the sacrifice of Christ would resound as countersacrifice. Christians lived in a religious milieu in which there were multiple sacrificial offerings. From the Acts of the Martyrs, or for example from the letters of Cyprian, we see how often Christians brought to trial were tested in their fidelity to the state on their readiness to offer sacrifice to the emperor. To proclaim therefore Christ as the one true sacrifice, and the Eucharist as the only sacrifice celebrated by his followers, was to swear allegiance to the lordship of Christ in preference to all other kinds of allegiance asked of them. This served to confirm their self-identity and their faith as a religious sect and a minority within the empire.

On the other hand, the situation of Christians changed radically after the edict of Constantine in 315 C.E. Now, the only sacrifice affirmed and proclaimed was that of Jesus Christ and the only celebration of sacrifice practiced that of the Eucharist. It is this common allegiance to Christ and the gathering in the basilica, or public forum, of the people of God (rather than the *populus romanus*) which were to assure public order. In this case, then, the remembrance of Christ's death in celebration as a sacrifice made it serve the social purposes of previous sacrifices in a more unique and comprehensive way, overcoming disorder, assuring a new order, and offering peace. Indeed, in the Roman canon it is apparent that the followers of the Church of Rome assumed the modes of address and petition (supported with gifts) to the emperor and his magistrates in their address to God when they gathered to commemorate the sacrifice of Christ, typified in the sacrifices of the just Abel, of Abraham their father in faith, and of Melchisedech, in his offering of bread and wine.

---

at the vigil but on Thursday. It still belongs to the commemoration of the death and resurrection of Christ, but its liturgical setting is changed.

Thus readings from the past show how the texts relate to and interpret different cultural and social experiences, and how through them communities express their relation to Christ. One can see the dynamic which is at work. The texts themselves certainly originated in specific settings and in some way address the issues of these settings. However, as written down they carry an openness to diverse ways of being interpreted and brought to bear on experience. The reading about the Paschal Lamb is about salvation through the smearing of blood and a meal of readying a whole community for departure, a departure that is a breaking out of slavery. Heard in the early centuries of Christianity, it was heard by communities who knew the shedding of blood and the fear of being bonded to false worship and domination. The texts were heard and brought to liturgical expression on the margin of society. In a later era, Christians constituted the community identified with the prevailing symbolic order. The text was no longer related to freedom from domination but to freedom from the disorders of sin that could disturb good order. Read within the context of social ordering, the images and metaphors do indeed have this potential. However, we never learn how they may have sounded to those who were subject to this prevailing order in such a way that their concerns and interests were not allowed social and symbolic expression. How might they have found the power of liberating expression in the story of the Passover or in the story of the binding of Isaac?

New Life through a Disrupted Reading

It is this question that we can see emerge from the situations of the poor or dominated today. Rather than assume a well-established and symbolic meaning of these stories that relates them to the imagery of Christ's atoning and sacrificial death, the power of the text in its narrative, in its imagery, in its ritual metaphors, has to be allowed to break forth. This is disturbing to the good order of the liturgical assembly that wants to take the ritual as determined by an ancient tradition and keep close to original meanings. Truth, however, requires such disturbance. It does not call into question the appropriation of the mystery of Christ which was effected through a particular type of intertextuality of Hebrew texts with Christian faith and New Testament texts, but it does ask whether in a new context this kind of reading is still viable.

In present-day churches, the reading of Hebrew scriptures breaks away from the traditional, and this can be exemplified in relation to these texts of the Paschal Vigil. In some cases, a new kind of typology emerges, more directly related to a people's struggle than to the spiritual effects of baptism or Eucharist. In others, the texts raise more jarring questions about God and about the redemption effected in Christ. To set the stage for such disruptive readings of ancient patterns of liturgical intertextuality, we can consider the interpretation of the Paschal texts in a Latin American, an African, and a South African context, respectively.

Latin America

How, for example, may this proclamation sound in the ecclesial communities of Latin America? What exists there is a situation of economic exploitation and political inferiority, as well as the cultural exclusion of the people of Indian and African origin to whom the pope addressed himself at Santo Domingo in 1992.[12] Within the Church, there is the movement, however compromised in recent years, of base communities among the poor seeking their liberation from this subjugation and finding impetus in faith in Christ and in their readings of the scriptures. This "liberation theology" has been given voice and form in the written works of theological scholars, but it did not originate there. In hearing the story of the Paschal Lamb, struggling communities may find promise in the redeeming power of the Lamb that shall save them from slavery and from death, and in the strength of its flesh that gives them provision for the journey of this exodus. The story of the binding of Isaac serves to build up their faith in the love shown by the Father in giving his Son, and by the Son in identifying himself in death with their own lot. In other words, the sacrificial imagery still plays its part and the two stories complete that of the Passion, but this happens within a narrative context which offers a plot that relates to the struggle for freedom of those who hear it.

A straightforward interpretation of the death of Christ as satisfaction for sin, or according to a divine mandate, is put in question by the interests of the situation. Read simply as types of sacrifice that illustrate the sacrifice of Christ, Exodus 12 and Genesis 22 are traduced and so is the Passion of Christ. The conflictual situation of

---

12. General audience, Rome, 21 October 1992; in *L'Osservatore Romano*, weekly English edition, 28 October 1992, 11.

the people in Egypt and of their efforts to seek freedom and cultural and political identity emerges to the fore and brings questions to how the death of Christ is to be seen. If it is seen only as a sacrifice of satisfaction for sin, assuring social solidarity or ecclesial solidarity, it is falsified. The attitude of Jesus toward the poor and toward established authorities and traditions exhibited in his death is brought to the fore from the place of these ecclesial communities. This calls for a new way of seeing what it meant for Jesus to shed his blood "for sin."

Genesis 22, the binding of Isaac, may in turn raise the issue of misguided religious ideals. Traditional Christian interpretations underline the obedience and faith of Abraham, who kept his trust in an inheritance because of God's promise, despite the death of his son. This illustrates Christ's obedience to the Father and the hope that remains even in this sacrifice. If the story is looked at from the side of a struggle for emancipation, people may be led to think of the losses of their children, either through early mortality or through forced migration. They find an invitation to hope in Christ even as this happens. They may, however, also find that Abraham's religious submissiveness is misguided, that it represents a misconceived sense of a divine pact. Children are not to be sacrificed. The future is not guaranteed by the willingness to hand one's children over to the inevitable, naming it as providence. The death of Jesus, his shedding of his blood, his "sacrifice," is protest against such religious idealism. Eating of the flesh of this Paschal Lamb, being one with this Son of Man and Son of God, spells hope for release from the sacrifices that social conditions impose. It does not teach submission "to God's will." The biblical text does not give an answer; it is part of a religious struggle about humanity's relation to God and God's to humanity. Instead of providing a type for an understanding of Christ's death as sacrifice, it brings questions to our faith in his death's redemptive power. The "revelation" given through hearing the text is given in the experience of the Spirit who allows people to respond out of their situation and in their emancipatory struggle to the offer by God to the world of his Son "made sin."

African Readings in the Light of African Religion

By way of contrast there are the meanings given to sacrifice in the oral context of eucharistic celebration at the proclamation of the eucharistic prayer in some churches in Africa, for example, Kenya, Nigeria, and the Democratic Republic of the Congo (in the so-called

Rite Zairois). While this does not touch directly on the Paschal Vigil, it allows one to see how the sacrificial interpretations of the Passion expressed through the appeal to Isaac and the blood of the Paschal Lamb play out in prayer. These prayers are composed in African style, derived from the rites and prayers of African traditional religions. They gloss the Supper Narrative by a strong emphasis on the shedding of blood and on blood pacts that bind people together in covenant. The language of offering used in the texts is strongly related to intercession and includes those purposes for which sacrifice is usually offered in African religions, that is, for a good harvest, for healing, for childbirth, for reconciliation, for the memory of ancestors, and for peace and unity within families and villages. In this way, the sacrifice of Christ is remembered as the one and only necessary sacrifice, and as the once-and-for-all sacrifice, that meets all the needs evoked in traditional practices. God's offering of his Son in sacrifice for us evoked in the reading from Genesis 22 and the blood pact of the Paschal Lamb both serve to bring out this relation of Christ's sacrifice to traditional sacrifices.

Postapartheid South Africa

On the other hand, the church in South Africa still lives in the aftermath of apartheid. While this new era has brought the abolition of the abhorrent laws of segregation and subjugation, it has also resulted in an explosion of violence, in the sense that this is no longer contained within the area of the former African townships. It has not been possible to overcome the excessive social and economic divisions within the multiracial population. In many ways, even among Christians, there is a continuation of ancestral rites, sacrificial offerings, and feasts. Some of these express the bonds between people; some of them are addressed to the hazards and miseries of people's lives.

There are people living in this postapartheid society who have been called out to identify the bodies of their dead sons. Some have witnessed to the Truth and Reconciliation Commission, such as mothers who were asked by police authorities to name only the charred remains of a dead body. Some are still called to the police barracks or to the mortuary, or even to the schoolyard, to take possession of the corpses of children killed in township violence. How can such persons be expected to react to the story of God's command to Abraham to sacrifice his only son, the son in whom all

the promises given to him and to his wife, Sarah, abide? A terrible
sacrifice has indeed been imposed upon them, but how can this be
said to be what God asks? Can the sacrifice of Jesus Christ mean
that mothers are expected to allow their sons to be sacrificed to
violence, or at least endure it as God's will?

Such interpretation is repulsive. A return to the text of Genesis
22 warns us that it is not to be taken as a desire on God's part for
the death of Isaac at his father's hands. It is the story rather of a
testing. Were Abraham to see his son dead, would he still believe
in God's promises? Or has his faith in God been totally invested
in the fruit of his own loins and the fruit of Sarah's womb? It is
not so much an act of obedience that is asked of him, as a faith in
Yahweh that may stand up against the disruption of his concrete
hopes. God in effect intervenes to give him reassurance, but we
are left to understand that even with the disappearance of Isaac,
Abraham and Sarah would continue to put their trust in God.

For mothers and fathers called out to view the dead bodies of
their children, there is no need to view this as God's will. Lament,
wailing, protest are all in order. What emerges, however, from the
story of Abraham and Isaac in the midst of this dread experience
is that God's promise and loving care do not fail, even here. It is a
love that is guaranteed through the death, violent death, and cross
of Jesus Christ. By his death, Jesus himself is a victim of social,
religious, and physical violence. He is one with the sons of those
mothers who have seen their sons succumb, seen them consumed as
a holocaust. The cry of Jesus from the cross is a cry that the child
can no longer utter but to which the mother may give utterance in
his place. It is a cry of grief and of deep-souled lament. It is a cry,
however, which expires in the word "Abba," Father; in the handing
over of his life to God, in whom trust is still to be placed in this
extremity. It will be for the community of disciples to aid a mother,
and to learn from a mother, as she passes through this horror to the
trust of the disconsolate in the God of Jesus.

What does the death of Christ mean in such a situation, when
the Passion is read against the backdrop of Genesis 22? It is a story
which speaks of dead children, of the dead children of the apartheid
and postapartheid era of this South African society. With these children, Jesus is one. He too is victim, not of God but of human beings
and their machinations, their efforts to support the unsupportable.
His mother too has received the body of her Son, rendered almost

unrecognizable by the blows dealt it. Son and mother cry out, in protest and yet in trust. Hope may be too strong a word; trust is possibly closer to the mark.

In short, to have meaning, surely this complex of texts and narratives at the Paschal Vigil must address the situation of structural and physical violence that has reigned and still indeed reigns. If it is seen in social settings as a countersacrifice, a protest, and a call for an end of the violence to which apartheid "sacrificed" the majority of society, or as the invitation to love that counters the tendency of elements of postapartheid society to "sacrifice" other persons by violence in the pursuit of their own identity, is there a new power of social transformation that emerges from these texts?

A World Unsettled

To look to the Northern Hemisphere, in Europe and North America we find that the sacrificial language of the Eucharist is somewhat muted. At the Paschal Vigil, the text from Genesis 22 is optional and often omitted in practice, and Exodus 12 is placed in some churches on Holy Thursday as a mandate of Paschal remembrance while Exodus 14 is given great exuberance at the vigil where the neophytes are to pass to the table through the waters of baptism. There is a suspicion of the meaning given to the death of Christ as propitiation for sin. There is also suspicion of the spirituality that drew people to "offer up" their lives in submission to the inevitable. In both suspicions, there is a suspicion of the image of God projected in such notions. Hence, especially Genesis 22 appears to be quite problematic. Even Exodus 12 is read more for its liberative than for its sacrificial message, and what is underlined is the command to share in a meal rather than the offering of a sacrifice. If Christ is taken to be the Paschal Lamb of eucharistic celebration, this is because the shedding of his blood and the communication of his blood are redemptive and not because they are seen to make satisfaction for sin. It is communion in this blood, communion in the saving act of self-emptying love, that brings redemption. We are to drink from the chalice from which he drank, eat of his table, first as recipients of mercy and then as disciples who commit themselves to love in turn, love even through a witness of pain and suffering, imposed by others and endured for others.

In several authors, and latterly in a letter of Pope John Paul II himself, we find attention drawn to the wisdom of the cross as an act of *kenosis* or self-emptying, sign and assurance of divine love. From a negative perspective, one could say that the oral transmission of these texts has under new circumstances suffered an eclipse. This too is part of the history of the transmission of written texts. From a positive perspective, one could say that seeing them as part of a liturgical tradition raises questions about how the death of Christ is to be believed and as to how faith in this death is to be lived out in face of the human, social, and cultural realities of a postmodern age. Texts that raise critical questions continue in a different way to be part of an oral tradition of exchange and quest.

In these last examples, we have seen situations in which the typological reading of texts is disrupted and in which understandings of the death of Jesus as divinely willed satisfaction for sin are rudely jarred. Yet from this disruptive hearing there emerges a new life from these texts, a life born in the midst of violence when there is the trust that not even this drives away God's loving, if hidden, presence.

Summary Plan of the Life of a Text

Drawing from these examples, the life that a scriptural text takes on through its oral transmission may be summarized through the following points.

First, the written text itself is produced within a given religious and cultural setting, which is always in part constituted by oral and ritual action. Being set in writing, however, it is distanced from its original setting and made available to other congregations and eras. This allows its transposition, in different modes, into oral context and exchange.

Second, it is set within a canon, given the status of a classic, within the community of faith. One of the early criteria for deciding what belonged to the canon of written texts was oral proclamation within liturgical actions. Hence being of the canon means not only that a book is to be respected as belonging to the record of divine revelation but that it belongs by its given designation to the oral and liturgical exchange of Christian communities.

Third, the text is in practice brought into such exchange by preaching, didactic teaching, liturgical proclamation, and liturgical citation within prayers. At such moments it and its interpretation are related to the life of the community and to the world in which they live.

Fourth, the genre of the text will command to some extent the place that it is given in such ritual. Story, prophetic proclamation, wisdom texts, laments, and prayers are inserted into celebration in different ways, at different moments, in different mouths. This becomes an active, or acted out, interpretation of the words.

Fifth, being related to the life and celebration of a community, written texts converge with the preunderstandings, interests, and expectations of such people. When transmitted to the next generation, they carry with them some of the life of their given or received interpretation.

Sixth, texts belong here and now to the living and gathered community of this time and this place, and their interpretation for the present comes from this fact.

Seventh, since reading and celebrating with texts are related to the concerns, questions, and interests of different communities, in different eras and different places, the practice of relating particular texts in celebration may be called into question. This may then result in a new and different configuration of texts.

Eighth, given this living, and lively, transmission, it has to be said that no text of the Judeo-Christian tradition can be called *sacred* in the sense that it is untouchable or that it has a once-and-for-all determined meaning. As several of the examples given show, texts are treated quite freely so that one may use the image of play, as with a game or a musical text, to express how texts receive life from their place in oral transmission.

Ninth, those texts survive best which have a rhetorical and poetic force. In their creative power, they both make connections with the past and are open to interpretations that point to the future that may arise out of the present that is being lived through.

Chapter Three

What Is Written, Is Written

W HILE THE FOREGOING is a description of the life of a text as it is affected by oral transmission and ongoing interpretation, one cannot gainsay the fact that it may sometimes be betrayed in the course of the process. Are there then any criteria whereby the justness of the interpretations given may be assessed?

Two may be mentioned, always with the understanding that the interpreting and self-correcting process never ends. These are what are called critical validation and ethical assessment.

The first criterion is a strategy that is called validation, as in the validation of a driver's license held for some time and now confirmed. Though it can be taken for granted that the functioning of the driver has changed somewhat, confidence is still placed in the original proven capacity to drive safely. On the other hand, should the license holder fail the required eye-test, the license is withdrawn. In the context of textual interpretation, this process of validation refers to the need to go back to a scientific exegesis of a text, with special attention to how it came to be and to its literary form, so as to see interpretations in their relation to this. This does not of itself settle the meaning once and for all, but it allows readers to compare the meanings which a text has acquired through the process of transmission to what can be derived about it through historical criticism and through attention to its literary form. It is only practice that allows us see whether any given interpretation has strayed so far outside these perimeters that it can no longer be seen as anything but a certain accommodation of words rather than fidelity to what is put forward by the text as written. None of what was said in the preceding chapter therefore means treating the text itself lightly nor ignoring the rules by which any historical and literary text is to be read. A text does have its subject matter and its mode of expression.

It is in virtue of these that it continues to have the power to speak to reality and to engage its readers.

The second criterion estimates how the meaning of a text comes alive in a Christian community by looking to the ethical orientation of life with which it is associated. The people's witness to the Gospel goes with its reading of scriptural and other texts and with its celebration of Christ's memorial. Liturgy is always the privileged circumstance for reading scriptural texts. It relates them to faith in Christ and to the life of the Spirit and to those rituals which express the identity of the Church. It belongs to the life of a people and so if in their ethical behavior they seem to wander from fidelity to Christ, there is an immediate suspicion about their reading of texts. If their behavior does indeed reflect the love of God and neighbor, if it does contribute to the common good and the order of divine justice, then there is an argument favorable to the rightness of their reading of the tradition. The meaning given to texts which have played an important role in forming Christian faith and the understanding of the Christian mystery has to be tested in this way.

Validating a Reading

Overview of the Process

In determining the subject matter of texts or the issues which they place before a community, considerable use is made of two methods. One is called the historical-critical method. This is the effort to reconstruct as much of the original text and the circumstances in which it was written as possible. The likely mind of the author, given the historical reality of the time, and the ways in which a text may have been originally understood are explored. It is also asked what social or cultural factors played a role in the composition and transmission of the scriptural message and in the impact which it had.

Thus for example in reading the Gospel of Mark, it is pointed out that the community for which it was written suffered much for its faith and had a highly apocalyptic expectation of the Second Coming of Christ. The predictions of the Passion by Jesus, couched in the image of the coming of the Son of Man, have to be put into this context. Of recent years, some doubt has been expressed about the possibility of knowing the mind of an author or an original audience, or even of being able to reconstruct their life-world.[1] Nonetheless, efforts of this sort have a bearing on how texts are transmitted and understood.

The doubts about the efficacy of the historical-critical method have led to what is called the method of literary critique. This suggests that it is the words themselves which need to be engaged, for whatever the writer wanted to say was said in words, and moreover the actual words spoken or written may convey a meaning and a power that go beyond what the writer intended or realized. The Gospel of John says of Caiaphas that he had spoken of Jesus not out of his own convictions but with words that had their sense and power because he was high priest for that year. As the spoken word can have more meaning and impact than the speaker knows, so the written word has a power and a life and an opening up of meanings beyond the intention of the writer. Anyone who has written realizes this in revisiting writings dating back some years, even if this be no more than a letter written at an earlier time of life.

With this in mind, it is important to attend to the literary code and the power of words, to the way in which texts belong in a longer written tradition, and to the ways in which texts intersect with other texts. This intersection comes about when several texts, perhaps of rather different literary form, are put together between two covers, as happens with the books of the Bible. It also happens when selections are made and then linked to one another in an oral or liturgical context, as happens all the time in the use of the texts found in a liturgical lectionary. How each text is read and interpreted will be affected by this connection of texts with one another.

A very simple example illustrates this. The parable of the vineyard in the Gospel of Matthew (Matt 21:33–44) is more powerful when it is seen in relation to the Passion narrative which the same Gospel contains. Further meaning is evoked when it is read along with Isaiah 5, the song of the Lord's vineyard, in the liturgy. A fictional story, a narrative, and a song are put together, each with its own theme and style, but together they complement whatever meaning is derived from each.

---

1. This is sometimes expressed through use of the term "distanciation." This means that a text once written takes its distance from the mind of the author, the originally intended audience, and the conditions of time and place under which it was written. See Paul Ricoeur, *Interpretation Theory: Discourse and the Surplus of Meaning* (Fort Worth: Texas Christian University Press, 1976), 43–44, 89–94.

In terms of the kinds of literary form found in the scriptures[2] and in liturgical readings, a general distinction can be made between narrative or story, prophetic proclamation, wisdom literature, songs or hymns of different kinds, moral discourse, legal discourse, and eschatological sayings having to do with the expectation of the coming of God's reign or of God's judgment.

First Sunday of Advent, Cycle A

An example from the common lectionary illustrates how important this is in a liturgical setting. On the first Sunday of Advent for Cycle A, the lectionary gives Isa 2:1–5, with the responsory from the pilgrim psalm, Psalm 122; Rom 13:11–14; Matt 24:36–44. Matthew includes both a story of the journey of Jesus toward Jerusalem and his eschatological discourse about the coming of the Son of Man. Isaiah 2:1–5 is a prophetic proclamation that looks to the advent of all peoples to the hill of Zion and their habitation in a Jerusalem from which the king will reign over all peoples. In its time, it belonged to the warfare between the people of Judah and surrounding nations. In one way, it foretold Judah's victory. In another, it looked beyond immediate history to a time when Yahweh would command the loyalty of many nations. The psalm that accompanies this prophecy in the lectionary is a pilgrim psalm, to be sung along the road by pilgrims on their way to the holy city. Romans 13 is a moral exhortation given to the Church by Paul, rooted in his interpretation of the role of Christ in bringing justification to all peoples. It declares conversion to him to bring a new day, a time in which light prevails over darkness. Given the place of these texts in the liturgy of Advent, they are associated with the Christian expectation of the coming of Christ and with the preparation for the feast of the Lord's Nativity.

When texts are brought together like this, narrative has a key role. It gives the plot around which everything else revolves, including the particular liturgical celebration. In the case of this Sunday of Advent, in a way the narrative is muted. Most of the text of the Gospel recounts a discourse given by Jesus to his disciples on the way to the consummation of his preaching of God's reign, a consummation to be brought about in Jerusalem. The narrative plot

---

2. For this, see Walter Brueggemann, *The Creative Word: Canon as a Model for Biblical Education* (Philadelphia: Fortress, 1986); and Paul Ricoeur, *Figuring the Sacred: Religion, Narrative, and Imagination* (Minneapolis: Fortress, 1995).

is, however, clear. From his ongoing and heightening conflict with some of the leaders of the people, Jesus has moved on to instructing his disciples about the end of time and the coming of the Son of Man. In the manner of eschatological discourse, the time frame of this coming is both blurred and open-ended. It has to do with things near at hand and with things farther down the way, even perhaps with things at the very end of time. All relation to time, now, henceforth, or at the final end, is to be marked by belief in the advent and consummation of God's reign in Jesus.

It is to this salvific sense of time and history that liturgy relates Isaiah's prophecy. The nature of prophecy was not really to predict the future but to alert the people to the ever-active presence of God's Word among them and to the awareness of his binding covenant. Faithful to this word and covenant, they could look forward to its continued fulfillment in their lives and in the lives of the nations. When unfaithful, the people could see themselves subject to God's judgment, as they could also see the Gentile nations subject to this judgment. The immediacy and urgency of the call and of the presence of God were often expressed by the prophet with words such as, "This is the Word of the Lord," or, "God says to his people," or, "It is the Lord who speaks."

In prophecies, the city of Jerusalem played a role because it was the great city of David, a city and a fortress that dated to the time of Israel's greatest prosperity and domination over other peoples. It was too the city of God's dwelling, the location of the Temple. It could be given a strong metaphorical and symbolic role in the proclamation of God's rule. All this is present in the liturgical text of Isaiah. The liturgy, however, now relates this prophecy to the consummation of God's reign in Jesus Christ and to the place among the nations assured this rule by reason of his birth as Son of God and Son of Man, and of his preaching, Passion, death, and resurrection. All time is affected by his coming and presence, and the liturgy captures this in its ritual and memorial prayer, which look to the final consummation of God's reign, an expectation which marks the life of every day.

Hymn or song is also a particular literary genre. These are words (and music) given to people whereby to take part in what is proclaimed, to embrace it as a living reality, to rejoice or lament over it together, and to stand before God in this response to his covenant, power, presence, and message. Chief among the types of song found in the Bible are the Psalms. The collection found there encompasses songs or hymns that belong in a variety of circumstances. There are songs of wonder and joy in face of God's marvels. There are meditations on his Law. There are laments for times of adversity, affecting particular individuals or the people as a whole. There are the gradual or pilgrim psalms associated with the worship of Yahweh in the Temple of Jerusalem, already anticipated in the walk to the city by those who will gather for the great feasts of the year. It is one of these which accompanies the reading from Isaiah in the Advent liturgy, and it accords with a sense of hopeful expectation.

Moral exhortation is not without its place, and an example of this is found in the excerpt from the Letter to the Romans. In the Hebrew and Septuagint Bibles, moral teaching belonged in three sets of conditions. Most basic is the exhortation to be faithful to the Law. There is also teaching on how to be faithful in times of adversity when hope may wane. Finally, there is the moral wisdom associated with belief in God's creation and providence as it is exercised and made visible in day-to-day life, as lived season by season, year by year, and through all the transitions of the life cycle. Paul is clearly concerned about how Christians live day by day and about their publicly visible ethical behavior. However, he relates all moral conduct to faith in Christ and to faith in the new day which has dawned in him.

What the Advent liturgy does in its selection of texts is to make them play off each other in conveying an awareness of the living presence of God's reign for those who keep memory of Jesus Christ and who celebrate the mystery of his birth in midwinter. How narrative and its plot, eschatological judgment and expectation, the prophetic proclamation of God's manifestation and victory, the hymns of pilgrimage, and Christian moral exhortation weave together can readily be seen. It is also quite evident that though one may be faithful to the scope and composition of these texts, they are taken out of one context and put into another, with implications for what they now mean.

Hearers of the Word

But how does this textual reading relate to meanings given to Advent over time, and always liturgically associated with such texts?

In actual fact, neither what is taken from a scientific reading nor what come to be accepted or established meanings of liturgies and liturgical texts are the once-and-for-all sense of the texts in question. It is the hearers, working corporately, who have established these meanings.

Advent and its biblical texts, such as those considered above, were understood in the time of Bernard of Clairvaux to refer to "the three comings of Christ," and this reading survived for a long time. The first of these comings was his coming at the Incarnation, the third and last his coming in judgment at the end of time, and the second his spiritual coming into the heart of every Christian. This interpretation was associated with a very linear reading of history and of salvation history and does not in fact represent a necessary meaning. It may indeed be the meaning given to this season and its texts by the Church in a given set of social and historical circumstances. One may not wish to see it as wrong, but one does not have to see it as necessary. The texts examined are not of their nature associated with a linear view of historical development. On the contrary, they are more readily suggestive of God's interruption of human history and of his unexpected interventions. Confidence in God's promise and in the memory of the Word Incarnate does not mean that we can expect the life of the Church to go forward in a steady development. It is always to be open to the new and always to see itself under the kind of judgment passed on it when it is tested in its fidelity to the preaching of Christ. Today's hearers of the Word may be more ready to interpret these texts in the light of this sense of divine action and human fragility, as it accords with their own experience of time and history.

The use of critical methods when applied to liturgy is intended to free the scriptures from imposed meanings and to get back to their intended and original sense. This itself, however, cannot bypass the fact that reading is done in context, by persons who bring given perspectives and given issues to their reading and hearing. Attention to the literary forms of texts and the power of their words and metaphors opens them more readily to a plurality of interpretations that meet the differing conditions of hearers, even while it sets a compass by which to navigate.

There can be a more critical approach to past ways of linking texts which is not judgmental in a negative sense. Awareness of the limitations of any interpretation is also an awareness of the power of a text to give rise to this way of hearing it, within the given conditions of a place or an era. There may be a wager that the finesse of attending to literary forms may give these texts a power that can enter the lives of present-day hearers.

Texts Revisited: The Paschal Vigil

That texts may be released from wonted interpretations and uses of the past and opened up to new ways of speaking and seeing can be illustrated by going back to the readings of the Paschal Vigil.

Each of the texts, Genesis 22 and Exodus 14, in its original form already embodies an inner dilemma and question. The way in which they have been used in interpreting the Passion of Christ raises an even greater concern and questioning. The texts have to be read not for information, nor for the plot of ideal worlds, but for the questions and horizons which they offer to a people who live by faith and hope, however well or poorly articulated. The power of these texts emerges fully when they are related to the moral imperatives of a lived situation, with due attention to their character and nature as texts. Rather than allowing the stories to serve as types of Christ's sacrifice, it can be asked what questions they raise for people who live by faith in this sacrifice.

Genesis 22

Genesis 22 provides a special case for examination. As already noted, within the celebration of the liturgy it became an allegory for the Father's gift of his Son in sacrifice. Since, however, it suggests that God gives an order to Abraham to sacrifice his own son, it raises a moral dilemma. Could such conduct truly be asked by Yahweh? Could Abraham truly be expected to find in such an action a way of expressing faith and fidelity? Despite the fact that the typological meaning is quite ancient, despite the praise for his faith given to Abraham by Paul and by the Letter to the Hebrews, when taken in itself for what it says the text raises problems both in itself and for its liturgical reading.

What is this text about? Taking the readiness to sacrifice and kill Isaac quite literally, some see in it a testing of Abraham's faith, while others take it to be a story of how Yahweh weaned Abraham from the religious practice of sacrificing the first-born, known to him from other religious systems, perhaps even those of his own personal and tribal background.

For still others, even though it is about a supposedly historical personage, the story is to be taken as a fiction, which speaks its truth precisely as fiction. It is not the narrative of an event that is to be taken factually. Rather it is meant to show that in the ethics of the covenant with Yahweh, fidelity may impose demands not provided by legal codes, and which may even seem contrary to them. Seeing it as this kind of narrative, the issue is not so much sacrifice as the larger demands of God's covenant. Fidelity to Yahweh asks of his followers that they give God precedence even over their kin, or over things to which the passing on of the Law may seem bound. The story of Abraham having to sacrifice his own son makes this point quite dramatically.

This last reading seems pertinent. It is quite difficult to get at any original sense of the text, if not impossible, but respecting the text means taking it at its narrative value. Listened to in this way, it does raise the question about what is demanded when a person or a community follows the road of fidelity to God's covenant and revelation. Our normal legal and established ethical boundaries do not cover this ground fully. Priorities are established which do not conform exactly to "natural" priorities. People are asked, not in an abstract way but concretely along the path of life, to yield personal, family, cultural, ethnic, and national priorities to the service of God's kingdom.

We see this illustrated or "parabled" in practice in uncomfortable ways. In serving their nations, Mahatma Gandhi and Nelson Mandela turned out to be poor fathers of their own families. Indira Gandhi in many ways exemplified the same thing as a mother, but somehow went against her mission when she started to give preference to her own sons over the national interest. The decisions of these leaders could not be grounded first and foremost in the good of their own families if they were to respond to their greater mission. Their stories may serve as parables of the kingdom and provide insight into the meaning of the story of Abraham and Isaac.

Rather than looking at it as a story "not to sacrifice children" or simply as a "testing of faith," Genesis 22 is a story which asks about "sacrificing children" when the practical realities of serving the kingdom, of serving God and Christ in those whose faces impose upon us, may demand that we shift priorities outside our kit and kin. This is a way of trying to respect the text as far as possible, and yet relating it to the mystery of Christ. God does indeed emerge as one "who sacrificed his Son," who sent him to contend with evil and to give priority to his witness over the saving of his own life. God himself, that is, gives testimony to an overwhelming love that does not fit the patterns that we associate with a "human" world.

For those who have seen their sons or their daughters, or their husbands or their wives, taken from them, there is here a vision that may not exactly comfort but does at least place God within the picture as something other than a demanding despot. For those who have to let these sons and daughters "be" in pursuing ways that imperil their fortunes or their lives, it asks a generous gift. To those who must put aside family priorities in God's service, it offers a communion with God in this giving.

In reading this text, we may move away from typology but yet have learned a way of reading a narrative that gives insight into the mystery of God's love in Christ and into what is asked of those who walk the way of discipleship, in communion with Christ and with the Father.

As this case illustrates, respecting the text does not mean relying on historical reconstruction, nor on ascertaining the original audience and looking for a message intended for it. It is rather to attend to the nature of the text as text, to take it in its proper literary form. Genesis 22 is a dramatic narrative, with mythical and religious elements, that speaks to the relation between a man of faith and the God who has made covenant with him. A contemporary congregation thus hears it as a drama, a drama which speaks to the reliance of faith on God's promises and to the ethical implications of living by a faith that directs the actions of one's life.

We have mentioned the horror of reading the story of Abraham and Isaac at a time when children are so readily commandeered as soldiers, left homeless, prostituted, slaughtered, in other words in so many ways sacrificed to society. A typological reading relating this to the death of Christ seems inappropriate. We have also commented on what issues the story may raise for those who follow the way of God's covenant in faith. In a setting of our times, the text may through its own virtuosity address other issues. Precisely in defense of these children, what may Christians be asked to give up of their own personal and family interests? Reading the Gospel of Christ's Passion, we may indeed see him as God's child identified with the sufferings of the world's children. What does this ask of us?

From this example, we may state a principle for interpreting scriptural texts within the liturgy today. It is to respect their character precisely as texts, to admit the doubts about established readings, to allow the weaving and interaction of different texts, and thus to consider the issues which they raise in relation to the mystery of Christ.

Exodus 14

The Paschal Vigil also gives us the story of the crossing of the Red Sea with its accompanying canticle of jubilation. Here also the typological reading of Exodus 14 does not seem appropriate, once it is recognized that as well as a story of a release from bondage, it is indeed a story of the slaughter of an army. It is a narrative about escape from bondage and deliverance from the people's enemies. The people saw God on their side, saw God as the God of the oppressed, and rejoiced in this deliverance. This was, however, bought at a great price of the killing of Pharaoh's soldiers. The issue is certainly that of the deliverance of a people from oppression. We can speak of God being on the side of the oppressed. Can we, however, rejoice over the bombing of Serbia in order to deliver the Kosovars? Can we be happy about the death of children in Iraq as the price of keeping Saddam Hussein in check? Rather than a song of jubilation over the drowning of Satan in the waters of baptism, we have to see from this narrative that those who are called to follow Christ have to ponder the ways of serving him in faith in a world of moral dilemmas. Related to the story of Christ's death and resurrection, we find that God served those in bondage in Jesus, that Jesus was one with the suffering, not through victory in war but through identification with the just who witness to the love and truth of God in the midst of human violence. This is a guarantee not of political victory but of a presence, a presence in which the Son of God himself, the messenger of God, the Christ of God, is made to suffer.

Both the story and the hymn have a long-standing tradition behind them of typological interpretation in their application to the triumph over Satan in baptism. In recent times, in Latin America, more attention has been given to the true nature of the story. It is about the liberation of the Israelite peoples from Egypt and their formation as one people on the land which God was about to give them, and of the destruction of their great enemy, through the might and the intervention of God. As a narrative, it contains a laudation and celebration of "holy war." For the oppressed millions of Latin America, it helped them to look to God in their hope for a more just society, in the desire to possess land themselves instead of having their work exploited for the gain of others. Though there was also the hope that those in power, those who practiced injustice, would be brought to order, Christian communities did not embrace holy war. Instead, they sought other ways of overcoming oppression and of calling their enemies to justice.

This gives some insight into how a Christian community may hear this story when it is related to the Passion of Christ and to the mystery of baptism. The story needs to be heard as a dramatic narrative and the song as one of exultation for the promise given and for the destruction of enemies. As a story, however, it does have to do with struggle and freedom and the horrors of war. It is hardly acceptable that people in a liturgical gathering remain insensitive to this. Rather than destroying the possibility of relating the story and the song to the Passion of Christ and to baptism, this more sensitive reading allows Christians to face the kind of issue which the story raises, in the light of Christ.

With faith in God as the savior of the poor and oppressed and in the kingdom inaugurated in Christ as one of peace and justice, we do expect an action of the divine Spirit that favors these. The appeal to holy war, however, rings false when related to Christ. There is therefore a sense in which Exodus 14 is a "contrast story." God's intervention in Christ is not expected to be of this nature. The way of Christ in preaching the kingdom of the Beatitudes and his testimony in delivering himself over to his persecutors in behalf of the poor is another way for God to show his "mighty power." For those asking for baptism "in the name of Jesus," there is the question of how they will serve the covenant celebrated at the Supper table and of how they will share Christ's stand for the suffering, the oppressed, the poor of this world. Instead of resorting to "holy war" or exulting in the triumphs (which are also the miseries) of war, those who keep memory of Christ need to explore other means whereby to be faithful and to serve God's kingdom. Such questions are raised by the "contrast story" of Exodus and are by no means out of place in a celebration of the Pasch. What needs to be changed liturgically, however, is the exultant use of the Song of the Sea. It is plain and simply inappropriate for a people who ought to be sensitive to the horrors of war and indiscriminate bombings. It might actually be more fitting to sing a response wrought from the Beatitudes in response to Exodus 14 or perhaps Francis of Assisi's hymn of peace.

In short, these three stories, of Genesis, Exodus, and Christ's Passover, may still come together in the Paschal Vigil, but their more traditional typological reading is too ambiguous, too fraught in our time with the wrong lessons. Taken according to their form as narrative, the Old Testament texts enter a world where many ethical issues about the defense of the oppressed are raised. The stories themselves spell out these dilemmas and invite us to ponder the fidelity of the baptismal covenant in face of them. In face of the cross of Christ, from the story of his suffering for sinners and in witness to God's kingdom, how do Christians respond to the kind of issues that the stories of Isaac and of the crossing of the Red Sea make us consider from God's point of view?

What is happening here is that the traditional process of connecting texts is followed but within a different perspective. The text is respected in its genre; the narratives in their proper meaning enter into the perspectives of the hearers; they respond to the interest of the readers that these bring from the world in which they live. The three narratives are, however, made to intersect, and the first two in a special way are related to the story of Christ's Pasch. Within the liturgy, they became the invitation to enter into the celebration of this mystery through baptism and Eucharist. They invite a reflection on what it means to live by this faith, to hand our lives over to God, in our own present world, with all its difficulties and dilemmas, as some of these emerge from the stories of Abraham and the passage across the Red Sea.

Praying the Psalms

Praying the psalms in liturgy brings its own particular issues and problems. The context of the Easter Vigil is quite a good place to consider them.

Once in the history of liturgy, the psalms were often proclaimed for hearing in a way similar to that in which other biblical texts were read. Their poetic quality, however, led quickly to their placement as prayer texts in the mouth of the Church and of the faithful. Fathers of the Church such as Athanasius and Augustine capture the sense of this usage when they speak of them as prayers of Christ, prayers of the Church, and prayers of the assembled congregation.

The psalter does indeed provide expressions of the heart in many different literary forms and to meet many different situations. There is the pure poetry of praise as in Psalm 103, the agonized lament of Psalm 22, the song of a pilgrim on the way to worship as in the Gradual Psalms from 140 to 150, the narrative psalm that sings about a story remembered as in Psalm 105. Early Christian commentators found many of these suitable prayers to place on the lips of Christ, as when Psalm 2 was taken to express the triumph of his death and resurrection or Psalm 22 his vigorous lament upon the cross. Once deemed the prayers of Christ, it is but a step to allowing the Church to pray these psalms with him, or even to him, once the sorrow of his suffering or the glory of his lordship is recognized.

In similar fashion, many of the psalms are found to provide word and sentiment to meet many a situation in which the Church or the faithful find themselves. In joy they may sing one psalm, in wonder at God's creation another, in affliction still a third, and when moved to recollection of times past a fourth.

Some psalms have also proved easily adaptable to song in particular liturgical seasons, as Psalm 90 has been traditionally used on Passion Sunday and Psalms 72 and 122 in Advent, or Psalm 8 on any feast where the wonder of the Incarnation is proclaimed.

Exegetically, some of this accommodated use causes embarrassment. What needs to be remembered is that it is their quality as poetry which makes the psalms so adaptable. Their expression of emotion and their rich imagery fit quite a diversity of situations, as will be found indeed with poems that written in one set of circumstances readily fit into others.

Some comment on all of this may be made by considering some of the psalms given in the common lectionary for use at the Vigil of Readings at Pasch.

After the story of creation as given in Gen 1:1–2:4a, the congregation is invited to sing Ps 136:1–9, 23–26. As originally composed, the psalm is a pilgrim psalm, to be sung on the way to Jerusalem for the Passover feast. It is the praise of God for his great deeds. Its core is a remembrance of God's work for the Israelites at the time of the liberation from Egypt and in bringing them into the promised land, their enemies conquered. The first nine verses are, however, a praise in wondrous awe of the work of creation, placing humanity in this setting, as described in Genesis. This is proclaimed as an act of steadfast divine love. This is why these verses are chosen at this point of the vigil and are concluded with verses from the end of the psalm which announce again the love shown in the works of creation and in the particular care given to humankind. The sense of the psalm is of course with the omission of the deeds done for Israel, but the section chosen certainly expresses sentiments of wonder, awe, and thanksgiving which any people may well feel in contemplating God's creative action.

The reading about the flood in the time of Noah, given in Genesis 7, is followed by the singing of Psalm 46. This is a hymn of praise for Mount Sion, or Jerusalem, as God's holy mount. There is a double appeal to the imagery of water. First there are the mythical and chaotic waters which threaten the city, against which God protects it and its inhabitants. But then there is also the peaceable river which flows out of the mount, refreshing those who look to it in peace and hope. It is quite clear why this follows the reading about the flood, which at the Pasch is offered as a simile of baptism. Those baptized are protected against the chaos represented in the flood, and they are refreshed by the life-giving waters of the font.

There may be some present hesitation over the singing of this psalm today, when its exegetical reference to Jerusalem is in mind rather than its baptismal symbolism. We know the troubled history of that city in the common era and what turmoil surrounds it today, with competing Israelitic, Palestinian, and Christian claims to it. Attentive to the chaotic history of the world as recalled by the flood story (rather than simply the baptismal symbolism), the psalm might well cause a contemporary congregation to reflect on this sad conflict and on what it means about relations between Jews, Muslims, and Christians, as well as on the constant merging of the political and the religious in humankind's story. This is not unsuited to the remembrance of the Passover of Christ, who in his Passion was caught in similar conflicts and whose self-emptying brought him into it for its redemption. Christians need constantly to ask themselves what it means to invoke the name of Christ in the story of our times.

A third example is the placement of Psalm 143 after the prophetic word of Ezekiel over the field of dry bones. The prophetic reading is intended to be symbolic of Christ's victory over death and of the life that is given to the baptized. Originally, of course, it is a prophecy over the reduced and lifeless state of the people of Israel in time of subjection to their enemies, as well as promise of God's intervention to give them life anew as a people. Psalm 143 is of its nature a somewhat generic prayer. It is a penitential psalm, an individual sinner lamenting the onslaught of enemies and crying out to God for salvation. In the history of the Church, it has been used in conjunction with repentance for sin and the doing of penance.

Once again, Christian congregations need to be careful not to reduce readings about Israel to Christian and sacramental symbolism. The invitation to lament and repentance in the psalm may well invite not only to sorrow for personal sins but to some corporate memory and some healing of memories such as required in the Jubilee Year 2000. As a congregation keeps memory of the Passion of Christ, it can ponder how religious instincts and ecclesial pretensions contribute to humanity's affliction, and indeed even specifically to the persecution of the Jews and to the present sorry state of the Mideast. Rather than a comfortable answer, both the prophecy and the psalm are an invitation to consider how our memorial of Christ's Pasch belongs to a reflection on the response of this Christian faith to issues in human history and in its present. The present includes of course what is to be done in face of those suffering from AIDS and famine, whose condition is indeed readily invoked by the image of the field of dry bones. The television screen may blunt our feelings, but it does not always lie about the facts.

These examples illustrate questions and possibilities of the place of the psalter in contemporary Christian prayer and liturgy. Their poetry is always evocative, but rather than sounds to be repeated they also invite a contextual reading and reflection, even as they are proclaimed or chanted.

Other Examples

Matthew 11:20–24

We can test these approaches further by taking another liturgical instance, already mentioned. Considered earlier was the liturgical reading of the woes on the towns or of those on the scribes and Pharisees from Matthew's Gospel (Matt 11:20–24; 23:13–36). If these woes are to be rightly considered and to become integral to a celebration of the Eucharist, respect for their true literary nature is pertinent. They are "covenant curses." That is to say, they are the reverse of the Beatitudes and are a declaration against those who refuse to live by faith in Christ and by the Beatitudes of the kingdom to which he testifies, in word and in his Passion. In Matthew's Gospel, both these texts parallel Matt 5:1ff., as counterpoint. The first set are spoken against those who refuse an ear to Christ's teaching, who set their hearts against the gift of faith. The second set are spoken against any who claim religious righteousness and replace faith in God's grace and action by reliance on their own works. However religious these may be, however exact their observance of ritual, they can only bring down a curse if they create an obstacle to true faith and to the service of the covenant.

Historical reconstruction of these passages attends to the course of Jesus' preaching and ministry and reconstitutes the nature of the opposition to him and its effects upon his story. In the drama of denunciation, Jesus himself appears in somewhat belligerent frame, and so it is asked whether he did indeed utter such curses. Their inclusion may well be a ploy of the evangelist to highlight the nature of his Gospel and to highlight also what in the religious world constitutes opposition to it. The woes sound the knell of a divine judgment which favors Christ and excludes those who refuse him from the kingdom. A reading which respects the literary character of the text sets aside the problems of reconstruction. It can take the curses as counterpoint to the Beatitudes and allow them in their role as counterfoil to pinpoint the true nature of the reign of God in Christ and to invite reflection on the human and even religious behavior that is opposed to it and that excludes people from the blessings of the kingdom.

Wednesday, Thirteenth Week of Year

The texts for this day in the Roman lectionary are Matt 8:28–34 and Amos 5:14–15, 21–24, with verses from Psalm 50 as responsorial. The Gospel text provides a good example of how to respond to a text when it is respected for its own genre, in this case a fictional story.

It is quite obvious in the case of the Gospel that it is a fictional narrative. Though it is about the historical figure of Jesus, the incident reported could hardly have occurred as described. In Jewish territory, there would not have been a herd of swine into which to cast the demons. If it is taken, as is unhappily sometimes the case, as a story of fact, it simply provides an exercise in explaining

the historical incongruities and fitting Jesus' ministry into an un-
likely scenario. Hence we have to ask what the evangelist wishes
to say about Jesus by telling this story, perhaps culled from current
religious tales of the time.

The story is about Jesus' confrontation with the demonic and
about his power to control and overcome it. The story of possession and expulsion makes this very graphic. Those who heard or
read the story are invited to have faith in Jesus' power. In one sense
it could be called story as parable. It serves to bring out the power
and nature of Christ's mission. It is of interest that the demons are
often among the first to recognize Jesus as the Son of God. Those
possessed by evil may not readily succumb to this messenger from
God, but when divine justice is presented in its truth and authen-
ticity, they are threatened. There is also reference in the text to the
"appointed time." As in all subsequent ages, early believers were
much concerned about the time appointed for the triumph of Christ
to be made manifest. The response implied in the Gospel is that it
is for his disciples to continue their preaching and their witness to
Christ. The appointed time is known only to God.

On this Wednesday of Year II in the lectionary, the Gospel story
is joined with a reading from Amos. This prophecy is a long tirade
against those, especially among the religious leaders, who are igno-
rant of the justice of God, however observant they may be about
religious practices. Israel is portrayed as a corrupt society, corrupt especially because no compassion or justice is given to the
poor and neglected. The two texts, Gospel and Prophet, invite a
congregation to consider the demonic in their own midst and in
their milieu. Where there is moral corruption, the demonic is at
work. Confronted by this, Christian peoples are asked to have
confidence in the power of Christ. They may not know the "appointed time," but they are to show forth the truth and the power
of Christ in their own action and testimony, with faith and hope in
his presence.

Liturgy for the Feast of the Epiphany, 2000

These comments on the meaning of individual texts in their
liturgical setting of the celebration of Christ's mystery may be
complemented by looking at the way in which several texts are
interwoven on a given liturgical day.

At the beginning of the year 2000, Epiphany was celebrated on the First Sunday of the year, 2 January, coming fast on the heals of the celebration of the advent of the millennium. Most countries had resorted to a tremendous and exhilarating display of light, with fireworks, the use of laser beams, Ferris wheels, and the like. Some few countries had gone to less expense, with simple candlelight to cast out the darkness, but such celebrations were in another way more impressive. The people gathered in the Polynesian islands had sent an old man and young boy out into the sea on a boat, the old millennium passing on its torch to the new, both journeying together into the dark ocean with the comfort of the light. On Robben Island in South Africa, the veteran of freedom Nelson Mandela passed on a lighted candle to the current prime minister, Thabo Mbeki, who in turn passed on this light to a group of young schoolchildren, who holding their candles at the midnight hour stood around to form a luminous configuration of the African continent.

In North America, as is usual of course over the Christmas season, the members of the congregation gathered for Mass had placed lights in their Christmas trees at home, had lit the Christmas candle in the window, and some had placed artificial lighting on the front of their houses or on their lawns. With their children, they had gone into the cities, into shopping malls, and wandered around neighborhoods, to see the seasonal display of lights. Thus they came together that Epiphany morning in the blaze of the Christmas and millennial light.

What would it be to "respect the text" of the liturgy readings on such a morning, and still let them speak to people hopeful in the light, enlightened as it were by what expressed the desire and intent of the human spirit at that dawn of a new century? In the common lectionary, these texts are Isa 60:1–6, with verses from Psalm 72, Eph 3:1–12, and Matt 2:1–12.

The reading from Isaiah 60 gives a pen-picture of the city bathed in the light of the rising sun of the dawn. It transposes this to a time when the people have been made free and have a reputation among the nations for justice, prosperity, peace. It depicts their neighboring nations (and indeed "all" peoples) as attracted by the fascination of this light, of this God-dwelt city and people, coming to it with their needs, their woes, their gifts, ready to place all their resources at the service of this peace and under the subjugation of Yahweh. In his letter, Paul exults in the simple fact that in Jesus Christ the plan of God, God's loving salvation, has been made known to the Gentile nations, that the Gospel is for all, that all will live in harmony under this Gospel, with this luminous revelation.

The Gospel text, the story of those who came from afar guided by the star to seek the King of the Jews, has developed quite a life across the Christian centuries. Even the translation of the word that describes them has a history. Very often they are known as kings. In contemporary translations they are called either magi or astrologers. The story of the kings had probably the longest standing in common Christmas folklore and piety because it represents power attracted by lowliness, wealth by poverty, the power of rule by the power of God exercised in the hand of a babe. Their very gifts of gold, frankincense, and myrrh interpret the mystery of the Christ child who is called to be the Savior.

Their kingship, however, does not seem to belong to the text as written, so how can the text be respected and yet take in the allure of this age-old story of the three kings? The imagery of light, the fact that the Old Testament story and the story of the Gospel have to do with the attraction and radiance of light, is the cue, an especially forceful one on this millennium morn. Both stories tell of how people from far-off lands, from outside the Jewish realm, are attracted by the light to the justice of God, shown in the one case in the peace of Israel and in the other in the infant with his mother, whose life is indeed sought by Herod in the presage of things to come. The personages in the story were in all likelihood persons who studied the universe, who explored the cosmic realms for the mysteries of the universe, and who had a particular interest in the luminaries of the night sky. They were seekers. They were people who sought wisdom in the plan and order of the universe but who knew well that they had to wait for the moment when the universe would reveal itself in the appearances of new stars and planets, and that to gain wisdom they had to be attentive to these revelations. Knowing the secrets of the universe would no doubt give people a wisdom whereby they could live in harmony with it and its mystery and in harmony among themselves. Those who arrived in Jerusalem and came to Bethlehem did not come together from one place. They represent different peoples, so that the story of the kings which depicts one of them as a Moor is true to the diversity of origins of the seekers of the Gospel story. All seek wisdom, all seek the secrets of the universe, all are obedient to its mystery. All are brought to the light of Christ by the radiance of the star's manifestation. Christ is the end of wisdom. He is God's Son and Word, the point of origin and the point of arrival.

On a millennium morn, people then hear this story of those who have been given the light but must seek the light. They have the light but will possess the true radiance of God only if they seek the light. All nations are indeed called by God; all are drawn to Christ as divine light, the light in virtue of which they may live together in harmony and wisdom. But the journey of all who seek the light, by whatever path, is to be respected. This year was proclaimed for Christians a Jubilee Year. Jubilee is spelled out as a year of reconciliation and of forgiveness. It is a year to seek further to live by the justice of God and to walk with all toward that justice, knowing that not all paths are identical. The Epiphany of God in Christ draws us, enlightens our paths, and sends us out to seek the light.

As people put lights in their homes but go out to see the lights, knowing by instinct that their light must merge with the whole array and splendor of lights, so to live by the light peoples of nations and churches must seek the light as it shows itself in others. The light of Christ shines in many places and ways. It merges with the light by which others live, whether by reason of religious traditions or by reason of an honest effort to follow the human instinct for the good. In their very adherence to Christ, his followers are invited, within the circumstances of the day and by a hearing of the liturgical texts, to seek with others for the light of the divine that may guide all seekers for truth and for justice.

Ethical Validation

Having considered the validation of meanings derived from texts by tracing them back to exegetical roots, we may now consider the process of ethical validation. In the first place, we can look at how some customary readings that are linked with liturgical celebration are called into question when their ethical implications are noted. In the second place, we will see how ritual helps to define the meaning of texts and their ethical consequences.

Public Morality, Scriptures, Liturgy

There is a rather well-known story of Pope John XXIII's intervention in a Good Friday liturgy in Saint Peter's Basilica. He had decreed that in the prayers of intercession marking that day, the

Jewish people should no longer be qualified with the adjective "perfidious." The canon of the basilica reading this text failed to omit the adjective, at which point the pope interrupted the service and ordered him to repeat it in the way now prescribed. John XXIII knew well how Christian attitudes toward the Jews were formed by liturgy and how much evil had been done against them over centuries in the name of Christ. In the sequence of liturgies leading up to the Triduum, the prayer is not an isolated text. During the final weeks of the forty days, the Gospel readings for daily and Sunday liturgies are taken from John. They depict the conflict and growing tension between Jesus and those whom the Gospel calls "the Jews." Early and medieval Christianity took this term globally and laid the blame for the death of Christ at the feet of the Jewish race and looked upon the Jewish people as Christ-killers. They castigated them even in their prayer.

Despite the action of John XXIII, the Good Friday reproaches based on Micah 6 are still in the ordinal for Good Friday. Because of the beauty of their melody they have an appeal. In singing them, congregations may think more directly about their own sinfulness than about the Jewish people if they are not inclined to be anti-Semitic and are focused on the sufferings of Christ for all humankind. However, to those sensitive to the power of language they are an embarrassment. Often they are not now used in Catholic communities. The *Book of Common Worship* of the Presbyterian Church (USA) published in 1993[3] tries to deal with this by addressing Christ's lament to "my people, my church," but so much of the story recalled so obviously has to do with the Old Testament and the Israelites that this does not resolve the problem.

The ill treatment meted out to the Jewish people by Christians over centuries is horrendous and is an awful background in European history to the attempted Nazi extermination. This in itself is enough to call the interpretation of the texts of John's Gospel as it is fostered by the liturgy into question. Some exegesis today suggests that the term "Jews" stands only for those leaders of the people who were Jesus' staunch opponents in the interpretation of the Law. Some historical reconstruction attributes a nascent anti-

---

3. *Book of Common Worship*, prepared for the Presbyterian Church (USA) and the Cumberland Presbyterian Church (Louisville: Westminster/John Knox Press, 1993), 288.

Semitism to the author of the Gospel, something which is prolifically amplified already in patristic writings. Another form of historical reconstruction looks into the part played by the Roman authorities in the execution of Jesus, to show that it is historically incorrect to attribute his death to Jewish persons. As remarked before, all historical criticism and reconstruction have their limits. Those concerned primarily with the text and its impact know that in public reading of the texts at issue and associated texts the way of referring to the Jews has to be tempered. The ethical validation tells us that long-standing interpretations are wrong. Consequences for the use of scriptures in liturgy must in time go beyond the omission of the adjective "perfidious."

There are a number of other examples of how ethical validation calls the liturgical proclamation of certain texts into question. Homophobia is fostered by the public reading of some passages about sexual morality. The proclamation of the household codes in some of the New Testament letters usually serves to enhance the subjection of women in societies dominated by patriarchal symbolism. If these texts are read, because they are in the lectionary, they need very careful treatment and explanation in order to remove the danger of misapplication in our present world. Some location of the texts within the time of their origin helps, but how they sound in the light of a developed ethic and a different cultural horizon probably needs to be stated quite explicitly.

In other cases, of course, a careful reading of and commentary upon a text can be ethically liberating. Thus the story of the healing of the woman who suffered constant hemorrhaging attends to the legal and ritual aspects of her situation. Her affliction was not only bodily. She was also considered ritually unclean, and this carried legal consequences with it. As already noted, Jesus' words and action include comment upon these codified attitudes. The story hence serves to call a congregation to look into comparable attitudes or rules in their own lives and societies. Proclaimed within the liturgy, it calls attention to how the Mass itself may ritualize differences and prejudices. From ethical consequences, communities reflect back upon liturgical behavior and the liturgical selection and use of scriptural texts.

The adequacy of liturgical renewal is always open to ethical testing. We need to be aware that this is so. Returning for an example to the woes from the Gospel of Matthew, when these curses are brought face to face with the Beatitudes it is clear that a definite ethical code is being proposed to Christians. This interpretation contrasts with a more legalistic kind of morality, not unknown in the life of the Christian churches. Which does more to serve God and human society in its pursuit of the good is what lies open before us, and it is this which will validate or invalidate the way of reading the Gospel.

Ritual Interpretation

Relating the Johannine readings about the controversy between Jesus and the "Jews" in close proximity to the ritual observance of the Passover contributes too readily to an interpretation that blames the Jewish people for the crucifixion of Christ. This is a warning that we always need to be alert to how ritual actions interpret scriptures, with serious ethical implications, since the ritual orders the world in which the texts are heard.

Thinking about the change of social observances in our daily lives, however mundane these may seem, brings home the point. My brother is a poet. In some of his lines, he shows a touch of whimsy. One poem in particular delights me, when he allows himself to be puzzled and elated by the absurdity of the fierce ethicist who urges that the invention of the tea bag had made a "dent in morality." With the title "The Collapse of Morality?" the poem reads:

> It's hard to say that or this is
>   a verifiable hypothesis
> but one I've heard enunciated
>   has left me feeling much elated
>   in wonder at its sheer absurdity.
> I can't help speculating where did he
> get hold of quite so quaint a notion—
> propounded too with such emotion!—
> as that morality was fatally dented
> the day the tea bag was invented.[4]

I too am elated by this ethicist who in his absurd defense of a custom displayed some instinctive insight into the broad ethical implications

---

4. *The Past Must Rise: Poems by Brian Power* (Dublin: Bayleaf Publications, 1999), 46.

of changing small but sturdily rooted customs in the breakfast room. There is quite truly an abyss between two worlds. There is that wherein, to receive a visitor, one goes through the routine of the meticulous and caring scalding of the teapot, the dealing out of teaspoonfuls (one for each drinker and one for the teapot) into the pot, the patting down of the tea cozy, and the leisurely wait at the table for the tea to draw while engrossed in conversation. Then there is the world in which a passing visitor is supplied instantly with a tea bag in a hot microwaved cup of water, while the two get down instantly to business. The difference is not between a moral and an immoral act but between two different civilizations and two different ethical universes.

Whatever the poet's intention, and peace to those who might well be disposed to laugh at the concept of the distance of an author from his text, the poem makes one reflect on the turmoil of inner emotion and outer custom when caught in a landscape that one does not recognize. It may be as small as a breakfast room, which is now deprived of all its customary markers so that it is hard to orient oneself or to know how to relate to traditions, to changes, to other people. I can allow my sibling poet his whimsy and his amusement at this gabbling ethicist, but I also hear in the poem images and metaphors of empathy with the plight of those for whom our quaint envoy speaks. The ethics implicated in the interpretation of texts and their impact on life is rooted in this perception of differing universes, with their symbols, customs, social order, and values. Obviously the one with the measured teaspoonfuls and the one with the tea bag are not treating their caller the same way. The drinking of tea has altered purpose and significance. They abide different worlds. Even if they have made no conscious moral choice about how to drink tea or how to greet a visitor, they subscribe to two different worlds in which moral choices are made.

A younger person who knew not loose tea may be adrift in reading this poem, not knowing this world of leisurely hospitality, with both its kindness and its taut social conventions that could be called upon to camouflage dis-welcome, for good manners can also play the part of hypocrite. This reader, if she pauses long enough over the image of teaspoons, may need some explanation about how to fill a teapot in order to grasp the contrast between worlds. Will she be given some new perception into human relations and the conventions of human encounter? Will the contrast allow her to think more deeply about the purpose of social, even the most trivially domestic, conventions?

When the conventions belong to public ritual, change may have larger implications. In the Catholic Church's liturgy at present, there is much disagreement over the Holy Thursday liturgy of the washing of the feet. The rubrics of the sacramentary prescribe that the one who presides should wash the feet of twelve males. The reason given is that the ceremony reenacts the action of Jesus at the Last Supper when he washed the feet of his twelve disciples. That there be only males, to the number of twelve, is related to what it is professed took place at the Last Supper, namely the institution of the Eucharist and of the priesthood in and through the twelve. On the other hand, it is known from history that at one time the Holy Thursday washing of the feet was indeed done in imitation of Christ but that it was a rite of hospitality, the washing of the feet of the poor in monasteries.[5] From there it entered into the liturgy. In some churches today, there is an attempt to retrieve this action and its significance, in one form or another. In other places, change is taken even further by including women among those whose feet are washed.

The symbolism involved has institutional and ethical consequences, the two intertwined. The key question is whether on this day it is appropriate to remember primarily the institution of the priesthood or the action of Jesus as servant, whose service is for all. Is the commemoration of the Last Supper on this day meant to highlight the role of the clergy in the Church, or is it better observed by taking this rite as a rite of hospitality, especially hospitality to the poor?

Involved in this is scriptural interpretation. How is the Gospel text of John 13 being read and interpreted in this ritual action? One kind of ritual reading gives primacy to the place of the twelve in the life of Jesus and in the ministry of the Church. The other takes the description of Jesus as servant, and his action of service, as its cue. In one case, the ethical implications have to do with religious respect for the ordained priesthood. In the other, what is put to the fore is the call to serve the poor and to practice hospitality in the loving service of others, in order to partake properly of the sacrament of

---

5. Peter Jeffrey, *A New Commandment: Toward a Renewed Rite for the Washing of Feet* (Collegeville, Minn.: Liturgical Press, 1992).

the Eucharist. To partake of the sacrament and to serve Christ with loving care in others are complementary, the one needing the other. More at the center of Christian liturgy, one can also see the link between the communion ritual in the Eucharist and the interpretation of scriptural texts connected with it. If the rite is regularly dis-inviting, as when the faithful are regularly not offered the cup of Christ's blood, the words of the Lord in the Supper Narrative are dis-interpreted. Though he says, "Take and drink," the ritual dis-offer says that the words mean something else. That was of course a common theological interpretation during the centuries when communion was infrequent and the accent was put on the offering of sacrifice rather than on invitation to communion. When Martin Luther had the words proclaimed aloud and in the vernacular, and followed them with the offer of the bread and the cup, the sense of the text was altered. In the Catholic Church at present, the approach to this rite is uneven. Recent directives try to make a large separation between the communion of the clergy and the communion of the faithful. Do Jesus' words then invite those assembled to different places at the table, or do they invite some to the table and tell others to wait until they receive the crumbs?

How the relation of the texts of the vigil already examined to ritual gives them specific significance is also clear. When the passage through the waters of baptism is related to the passage through the Red Sea narrated in Exodus 14 with its accompanying song, this is an open invitation to read the story for its baptismal symbolism and to unfold moral and ethical implications from this. Such an approach is amply demonstrated in patristic mystagogical catechesis. Paul in his Letter to the Corinthians had already displayed the ethical implications of the Lord's Supper inherent to the sharing of the one loaf and the one cup. Augustine developed this considerably in his instructions to neophytes during Easter week.

Modern concerns with solid exegesis make some of these interpretations questionable. All that we have said about Exodus 14 suggests how ill-suited it now is to baptismal symbolism, because of the deadening of nerves to human catastrophe that it may bolster. Exegesis of John 13 also suggests that relating the text in a strong way to the place of the twelve in the early Church, and so the priesthood, misses the point of the story, which is meant to bring out two things: the messianic imagery of the servant and the new commandment of love. Placing the laments of Christ on the cross in close conjunction with texts from John about the conflict between Jesus and the "Jews" only serves to increase Christian dislike for the Jewish people.

Such examples call for greater ritual care lest we deform scriptural texts. The matter becomes more serious when we neglect the consequences for public morals of certain interpretations that are related to liturgy.

Conclusion

In this chapter, the main concern has been with respecting the scriptural texts proclaimed in the liturgy and not subjecting them to allegorical or typological or moralizing readings. In a way it could be said that what has been asked is, What place is there for solid exegesis in interpreting liturgical texts? Attention to both historical criticism and to the literary form of texts was seen to have its purposes. The relation to the ethical implications of any interpretation was offered as a way of validating interpretations that can go along with this exegetical analysis. It was also said that however exact attention to the text in itself, the ritual action orients the meaning given to it by a congregation. In all of this the response of the hearers is at issue. Thus we can pass on to the importance of context in responding to what the liturgy proclaims and enacts.

Chapter Four

Echoes of the Word
at the Cusp of the Millennium

THE WORD OF GOD resonates within a social situation. It relates to a people's vision of life and to the values which they hold. These are inherited from culture but are always shifting with changes in living conditions and with the kind of relations one society has with another. The words of the Gospel and of early Christian writings were addressed in their time to a people of a Jewish heritage, in the first place, and to people inhabiting Greek cultures of wisdom, in the second place. The memorial of Jesus, the Christ, was an open challenge in both cases to a renewed vision, in the light of the relation of God to the world revealed in him. God, being Father and Spirit, was revealed in the world in the Son, the new law of self-emptying love by which the world is redeemed. Not only did this open eyes to the divine presence, but it also awakened believers to a constant expectation of divine advent.

To express what the proclamation of this Word means in later ages, one could use the example of an echo. An echo is heard when a word thrown out into the clear reverberates and returns. It is recognized as conforming to the original sound of the voice, but it has traveled across space, and the sound on return is new, marked by the places encountered in its progress. The Word of God given in the scriptures is like that. It is a word that was launched into the world and continues to be launched in different settings. As it echoes off new surroundings, it returns with a new sonority.

One wonders if it is possible to catch the rebound of this word in our time, this being such a complex period of human history. On the one hand, the entire world is linked. The globalization of politics and commerce, together with the ease of travel and ever-advancing means of communication, connects all parts of the earth and all peoples. On the other hand, people are confronted more readily by differences. The flattening of cultures and peoples into workable schematizations and structures of thought and organization, the imperialism of European colonization, and the commercial dominance of American society have been rendered suspect. Peoples whose human, civil, economic, and cultural rights have been subjected to external domination realize that they cannot have a just part in the communities of the future unless they retrieve and formulate their own heritage. This is not a reversion to some original state of innocence and expression. It is the search for an expressivity that will allow each person and each segment of society to be partners in a political, economic, and cultural community of greater proportions and that admits both interaction and diversity.

It is often stated today that it is impossible for people to walk toward the future without attending to the "other." Within our human communities, we cannot expect a homogeneity of outlook. Nor can we any longer suppose that all have the same cultural background and the same values. No nation or religious group can flourish by dominating others. It needs to expand its own horizons to include interaction with these "others." This is an enrichment of humanity, of each people, of every religious tradition. Furthermore, this gaze into what seems an infinite number of horizons serves to awaken the mind and the heart to an infinite transcendence. Human communion can be truly achieved when beyond the openness to others, there is a faith of some sort in a power, goodness, and truth that transcend human exchange. Indeed, this exchange is but a participation in the ultimate transcendent, however this is named.

For the hearing and interpretation of the scriptural Word, this means being able to hear the echo of that Word as it is proclaimed in different contexts, even while it invites to a communion that transcends all boundaries. Its interpretation involves respect for the Word in its content and composition, its relation to the social and cultural realities of the community that hears and receives it, and what it says in the liturgical context in which it is spoken. It invites a readiness to be drawn beyond human life into a communion with God where humans find a love and a oneness beyond imagination.

Life-Reflection

The interpretation of the text opened up in liturgy is able to lead to a prolonged reflection on what the liturgical scriptures mean to human life, in context. The liturgy offers the horizon, gives assurance to faith, and opens up issues. Liturgy itself is not the place for critical analysis and planning, but it must be in touch with lived existence and with the ethical provisions and decisions that people are called upon to make.

The example of the curses of Jesus in Matthew's Gospel looked at in an earlier chapter may serve us again. We noted the parallel between this pericope, the Beatitudes, and the scene of the last judgment. Through this paralleling of texts, we saw that the issue of the text was what blinded people to the conditions of the poor and the service of the poor. As told in the Gospel, the audience to Jesus' words, those cursed, were blinded by their way of reading the Law and the Prophets in their promotion of the privileged place of the interpreters of the Law in Israel. An ideology of ritual religious service and the image of a God who is best served in this way prevented them, for example, from hearing the injunctions of prophets such as Amos and Hosea.

A contemporary congregation may well have some members who are zealous about ritual observances. Parish ministers are well acquainted with those who watch liturgical performance with eagle eye to catch ministers out in some ritual fault. However, this will not be the major concern of the average (granted that there really is no such thing) congregation. For most, the question will be what deafens them to the injunctions about love of neighbor or at least hinders them from their implementation in neighborhood and society.

The hard questions have to be asked: What happens when families of diverse ethnic and cultural backgrounds move into a neighborhood? What keeps us from seeing them as neighbor? The answers may be cultural prejudice of the sort that places one's own above others. It may be that these people are seen as "different" and so difficult to get along with. It may be a moral attitude that is too wedded to particular commandments and not open to a larger picture of the community of disciples and its pursuit.

Another example would be the reading of the story of the binding of Isaac in a community that suffers from the poverty of its children, perhaps even their exploitation. In the story, they will hear how

Abraham was ready to subordinate the interest and life-expectancy of his son to the interests of a covenant with Yahweh rooted in tribal practices. They will know well what it means to put children below larger interests. They may do so themselves at times. They will have seen others do this. What has to change? How may they themselves find the strength and the enterprise to take initiatives toward change? How does the remembrance of Christ as Son of God who gave himself over willingly to the combat with evil, even with death, give them a sense of their dignity and a sense of hope? In conjunction with Genesis 22, they might well read the story of the trial of Jesus in the desert, of his conflict with Satan. His was not meek submission but strong combat. Too often, as in the AIDS crisis, poor people are made the subjects of investigation, exhortation, and a Western-style education about cause and effect. From their own traditions, values, and ways of doing, they can begin to draw resources, as Jesus drew on the prophets and on wisdom literature in his interpretation of the Law.

Concretely, this pursued reflection upon the scriptures is a matter of allowing it due time and giving it due preparation. In his exhortation on the observance of Sunday, Pope John Paul II remarked that the meaning of Sunday is not exhausted with celebration of the liturgy. It is a day to be given to things spiritual and to the promotion of human life according to the Gospel of Jesus Christ. There are places in the world where people give over the day to gathering for liturgy. On one occasion, when in an African country, I was invited to accompany a priest to a celebration of the Eucharist which he said was scheduled for 11 A.M. in a rural community. In fact, he made a point of being present well before the hour. People were already there, singing, talking, catechizing. Others kept arriving until about two hours later, when a woman informed the priest that "everyone who is going to come has come." In the meantime, the priest had occupied himself hearing confessions, teaching catechism, talking about the scriptures with some of the people, and joining in the singing. Needless to say, the eucharistic celebration itself took a few hours. On another occasion, in the Philippines, I met with a community of agricultural workers who met at 4 A.M. on Wednesday morning, before going out to the fields, in order to discuss the scriptures for the following Sunday and to see what they meant to them in their lives, which included a lot of injustice and a lot of struggle.

Western peoples are generally so programmed that this kind of thing does not happen. There is a way, however, in which some communities do prolong Sunday reflection and worship into the week. They take the bother to get somebody to explain the biblical books which are being currently read. They meet in small faith communities to share scriptural reflection, mutual encouragement, and prayer. If pastors take part in some of these groups, they in effect prepare their Sunday homilies with the backing of the people's reflections.

Another matter to which to be attentive is the constitution of the liturgical assembly. Our congregations tend to be very homogenous because our neighborhoods are homogenous. The ideal of a Christian assembly, however, is that it gather all who are baptized, from whatever walk of life, from all states of life, from all the cultures represented in the make-up of city or country. If people of one zone of the city were to meet with people of another, the questions brought to the hearing of the scripture would be quite diversified. To revert to Genesis 22, in the United States the answers to what is happening to our children would be quite different in an African American neighborhood, in a Hispanic neighborhood, in a Chinese neighborhood, and in an Anglo neighborhood. A way of bringing these Christian communities together, practiced in some of our parishes, is the twinning of parishes. In such a way of doing things, groups from one parish visit the other for scriptural reflection, to talk about common concerns or about social issues, and they also visit for the Sunday liturgy. This represents some effort, not supererogatory but necessary, to bring Christians together around the one Gospel and in the celebration of the one liturgy. In effect, doing this kind of thing is the wisdom of the people at work in their response to Jesus Christ.

To look at this connection between scripture, life-reflection, and liturgy more fully, we will consider how the interests and concerns of a congregation have an impact on how they hear and celebrate what is proclaimed. After some general comment on this, we can look at several, quite specific and quite diverse, situations. In every instance, we will discuss the possible response to the same set of texts, taken at random from one particular Sunday of the year.

Text and Life-Interest

Interpretation and Context

It is prosaic and matter of fact to say that texts are read in specific contexts. It is more complex to work out how this affects the way in which a text is interpreted and appropriated by a community.

In spelling out and evaluating the relation between interpretation and context, several things may be kept in mind. First and foremost is the fact that people are caught up in what is at hand, namely, those external realities that constitute the surroundings and the conditions under which they live. There are the geographical surroundings and the physical conditions of life. There is the use of artifacts for doing daily things. There are the economic conditions under which people live and the impact on them of their environment. There are the social differentiations which have a bearing on social and community realities. To be fully "there," people must needs be more attentive to these factors and to the relation between them.

Living in time and with the experience of change, human mortality will always command attention, both in terms of its brute fact and in terms of the meaning given to it, or of the prospects of survival beyond death. Communities look across time to what we have received from those who went before us and how we honor or maybe repudiate their memory. Each generation is likewise called into question over what it passes on to the future and more specifically to the next generation.

Religious horizons and traditions emerge and take root within this complexity of life. Hence there is a wide range of life-conditions to be taken into account in discerning the meanings which a community takes from its scriptures, especially those which are proclaimed time and time again in public services. What are the social and economic conditions that determine how people live, with what measure of struggle, what measure of comfort or ease, and what life-expectancy? What kind of social relations dominate in this time and place, and how is the human person valued? As people receive the impact of this life-situation, what are the symbols and rituals that gain response and appeal to the affective bonds that hold people together through some sense and expression of the common good? Answering this means attention to traditions, to stories from the past that shape attitudes to reality and to life, and to afterlife. What values, what views of the world, of life, of human being, prevail and influence how things are perceived and understood?

Every person and every community brings some interest, in the sense of concern, to the appropriation of what is proclaimed in a text and a ritual. They may not be greatly conscious of this, but they do have an interest in seeing the prevailing conditions of life stabilized or, on the other hand, changed.

Missionaries, for example, who encountered peoples who practiced polygamy instinctively and by disposition wanted marriage celebrated in such a way that society would be aware of the Church's prohibition of this practice. The Genesis story of the first man and woman and Jesus' citation of this story stood them in good stead. They could also hold up Solomon as a model of the evil effects of polygamy. In another instance, those who want to foster religious vocations make ready use of the story of the rich young man in Matthew 19, even though it is obvious that the text on its own historical-critical and even literary merits is not directed to this purpose. The matters, however, with which it deals can well be incorporated into this kind of life. Another use is made of the same text by those who want to promote a greater social equality and justice, since it pinpoints the obstacle that the possession and acquisition of wealth may be to hearing the Gospel of the kingdom.

Bothering to read a text at all, unless it is done out of some sort of ennui, to fill time and gaps, means giving it some value, either because tradition has done so or because entering a different culture and context it seems at first hearing to offer something new, some renewal. This is what is called a fiduciary reading, a reading done with confidence in the world that the text opens in front of the reader and in the questions about life and death, about the human person, about cosmos and about God, which it poses.

There are then a number of components to the reading of texts in context that encroach on the liturgical practice of intertextual reading: (*a*) "Being there" or being attentive to the surrounding life-situation; (*b*) the impact of tradition, history, culture, the influences at work from these sources, and the questioning of their impact; (*c*) specifying or spelling out the interest that arises from the situation in which people live and that is brought to the reading of the text; (*d*) putting the text into conversation with a new set of questions and referents, with confidence in what the text gives or offers, in hope; (*e*) in Christian tradition, bringing texts into the personal relation that a community and its members have with Christ and the Spirit, expressed and vivified within liturgical celebration, its rites, symbols, and language.

Thirteenth Sunday of Ordinary Time, 2000

An example will serve to illustrate how this works out in practice. This is taken from the readings for a particular Sunday in the year 2000 in the common lectionary. These will be considered first for their content and form. Then it will be asked how this word might be preached, prayed, and received in a variety of different congregations, while always expressing faith in the one Christ. The Sunday chosen is the thirteenth of ordinary time, according to Cycle B of the lectionary. It is chosen for the simple reason that it is the Sunday occurring at the time of this writing.

The texts, found in Cycle B of the lectionary, are as follows:

Wis 1:13–15; 2:23–24,[1] which is about the spiritual death brought into the world through the devil and about the human imperishability ordained by God, the Creator;

2 Cor 8:7–9, 13–15, which is an exhortation from Paul to give generously to the collection for poor churches and declares that Christian generosity is modeled on Christ, who though he was rich became poor for our sake;

Mark 5:21–43, which narrates the cure of a woman suffering from constant hemorrhage, and the raising of the daughter of Jairus, ruler of the synagogue, ending with a command not to tell these stories, which are stories of Christ's power (which is inherent in him) and of faith in him.

Respecting the Text

What may a simple attention to literary form and the use of words and expressions tell us about the content of these readings? It is usually wise to begin with the Gospel, since this is both the climax of the liturgical proclamation and the reading that casts light on the placement of the other two.

The Gospel of the day is a narrative that indeed takes in two stories, the one of healing and the other in all likelihood of a restora-

---

1. The common lectionary allows for the substitution of 1 Sam 1:1, 17–27, which is David's lament over Saul and Jonathan, killed in battle.

tion to life.[2] As a story or narrative, it is focused on the power of Jesus and on the faith asked in him of those who turn to him. It draws readers or hearers into a drama. Their readiness to follow the plot of the tale is what draws them into the issue and into what the story says of life and death. It is a story of how Jesus is faced by these issues of illness and death, a story told in very human fashion with rather cherished details that enhance its appeal. Of the woman suffering from hemorrhage we are told that recourse to doctors brought no relief and that she had lost much money to them, even though they could do nothing for her. We also learn of her attempt to be cured while unnoticed and of her fear when called out of the crowd by Jesus, though the disciples find his own question crazy. The woman's predicament of course is not only physical illness. Because of the blood flow which she suffers, she would be considered unclean, and this would itself have kept her anxious to be unrecognized in the crowd. In calling her out, Jesus is not simply causing her embarrassment, though her first reaction is fear. He is making his own implicit comment on the rules of law about impurity. He frees her from both the physical and the ritual burden under which she suffered.

In the house where the girl lies dead or in the extremities of illness, we hear of the lament made over her and of the scorn which those around cast on Jesus. We also are given the touching detail of Jesus' admonition that she be fed once she is restored to life.

In their richness of detail, the two stories and the narrative as a whole respond remarkably well to many a human situation. In its deep plot, however, the narrative is about the power which Jesus possesses as the Messiah and about how to respond to him in faith. Not only does he have healing powers, as many another prophet may have, but he himself is the source of that power which gives dominance over life and death. Even to touch him, as the woman did, is to experience him in this way. On the other hand, neither the ruler of the synagogue nor the woman benefits from this power without faith in him, in what he is, and in what he has come to do. His acts are witnessed by the disciples who are to be the witnesses to his death and resurrection, and none is to be told these stories who

---

2. Some exegetes suggest that the girl may not indeed have died but that a cure in the last extremities of life is a sort of giving back to life and of restoring the child to her parents and her kin. For the point of the story, whether she was indeed dead or only close to death does not seem that important.

has not attended well to the predictions of his suffering, death, and resurrection scattered through Mark's Gospel. That is the meaning of Jesus' admonition not to noise these works abroad, where they may be misconstrued so that his whole purpose in proclaiming the reign of God and giving witness to it may be jeopardized.

The reading from the Book of Wisdom is meant to be a foil to this. It is a foil because it raises the issue of attitudes to death and of hope in a life that does not end. As far as the book is concerned, the only death that undoes is spiritual death. This is the death which comes from sin, that inner attitude to the things of others, to other persons, to life, and to human mortality that separates persons, or even cultures, from God. Even when the innocent are seen to die, put to death perhaps by others or at least dying in ignominy, the person of faith is sustained by the belief that God has made humans to be imperishable and to live with him forever. Inherent to the efficacy of a piece of literature such as Wisdom is that it concerns not the great feats of human genius but everyday life. With what feelings and beliefs and attitudes do people attend to daily realities, to the wonder or the hunger that they encounter day by day, to the realities of sickness and health, of human passage, of birth and death, that constitute the pattern of the daily life of any family or community? Placed then as a foil to the Gospel, this reading creates a context in which the Gospel is heard and interpreted.

On many a Sunday, the epistle does not readily fit with the other two readings because of the way in which the lectionary selection has been done. This Sunday, however, it completes them in a rather remarkable way. What is the Church of Corinth, whose members are relatively prosperous, to do about the want and hunger of the people in other churches? Paul has proposed taking a Sunday collection from which to aid them. This itself has very concrete implications for all concerned. What is striking about this passage, however, is the way in which he gives a deep theological grounding in faith in Christ to his very practical requests. The Corinthians are to be inspired in their generosity by the divine example. Christ emptied himself of his own riches to come to the redemption of impoverished humanity. This acts as a kind of commentary on the Gospel reading. None can have true faith in the power of Christ in human life and in his power over death who does not believe in the mystery of his suffering and death. In short, the reading from Paul serves to make the mystery and the wisdom of divine *kenosis* the metaphor whereby to crystallize the import of the Gospel reading for the congregation.

The Eucharistic Liturgy

These readings are heard by people who engage ritually in the liturgy of the memorial of the death and resurrection of Christ. They are carried into this liturgy by the way in which the mystery of Christ is portrayed in the Gospel. The faith in which they invoke the Spirit and receive the gifts of Christ's body and blood is formed by the way in which the three readings focus on the wisdom and the love shown in Christ's self-emptying.

The reading from Paul serves to bring light and attention to what can be a routine part of any Sunday celebration, namely, the collection. This accompanies the offering of bread and wine. In putting their lives before God, in thanksgiving, and in the hope of blessing, in the bread and the wine the congregation also bring forward what they are ready to share with the Christian community and beyond it with those who are in want. It is to this very thing that Paul's words are addressed, and in a way which shows how integral this action is to the mystery which is liturgically celebrated.

Response in Context

We can ask then how the texts of this particular Sunday might be heard and received in a number of different contexts that prevail at the cusp of the millennium.

The Contemporary Euro-American Scene

During the week preceding this Sunday, there were three significant items in the news media. First was the announcement that the entire human genome had been sequenced, spelling out the 3.1 billion chemical letters that make up human DNA. Naturally there was much speculation about what this would permit by way of controlling illnesses and prolonging human life. The second item of news, much in contrast with the former, was the publication of a UN-sponsored investigation into the spread of AIDS across the world. The predictions of the rate of mortality within the years to come and its effects on entire populations were drastic. While AIDS affects primarily the African and Asian continents, the Western world is also implicated since it is the primary supplier of medical aid, whose distribution is much subject to the laws of commerce and profit that prevail on the global scene. The third news story concerned the threat by forest fire on a nuclear site in the State of Washington, making viewers and readers aware of the fact that the products of human ingenuity are still subject to the perils of nature and to human carelessness.

These three items of news summarize in their own fashion the way in which the advanced society of Europe and North America vacillates between what is dubbed the modern and the postmodern. The modern stands for progress, human genius, the power of reason and intelligence, and the capacity to affect standards of living and the very possibilities of life itself. It is often noted that along with this human progress there goes a separation between faith and reason, the sacred and the secular. This may explain to some degree the waning of religious practice and devotion on the contemporary scene. On the other hand, it posits a particular challenge to faith if it is to allow for the place which human intelligence and its inventions have in a view of life and of the world dominated by faith in God and in Christ.

Of this *modern* world, Pope John Paul II has said in his letter of 1998 on faith and reason:

> [A] rapid survey of the history of philosophy, reveals a growing separation between faith and philosophical reason. Yet closer scrutiny shows that even in the philosophical thinking of those who helped drive reason apart there are found at times precious and seminal insights which, if pursued and developed with mind and heart rightly tuned, can lead to the discovery of truth's way. Such insights are found, for instance, in penetrating analyses of perception and experience, of the imaginary and the unconscious, of personhood and intersubjectivity, of freedom and values, of time and history. The theme of death as well can be for all thinkers an incisive appeal to seek within themselves the true meaning of their own life. (*Fides et Ratio* [FR] 48)[3]

---

3. For an English translation of this letter, cited here according to the paragraph numbering of the original and of the translation, see Pope John Paul II, *Fides et Ratio: Encyclical Letter on the Relationship between Faith and Reason* (Boston: Pauline Books & Media, 1998).

What is in a rather vague way called the *postmodern* calls into question the human power to improve life, the possibility of relating one situation or story to another, and the ability to see coherently into the future. It points out the evils that go with the inventions and discoveries of the last couple of centuries. The foremost example of this from recent history is the operation of the Nazi regime in Germany and how it used science and technology in its attempts to exterminate the Jews and other unwanted groups of persons. The second of the news items above also illustrates the side of human nature which misuses or abuses what humans invent, since it tells how much the profit motive affects the use of the medical powers that are in human hands. The third item, about nature's threat to nuclear plants, raises the question about humanity's place in the universe: despite human ingenuity, are we not still ineluctably subject to the greater forces of nature and indeed in the end a rather insignificant item in this awesome universe?

Such questioning by no means implies an immediate recourse to belief in God but more readily raises the question of meaning itself: Can we truly find any meaning in the world or in human life beyond whatever we encounter or succeed in living day by day? Is the appeal to God not itself an illusion? In short, postmodern doubts about human life and its place on earth and in the cosmos are raised by the perceptible limits on human achievement, even at its greatest moments, by the reality of violence and of inequality, and by the perceived insignificance of human life in the entire scheme of things in the universe. Of this *postmodern* tendency, John Paul II says in the above-quoted letter:

> Our age has been termed by some thinkers the age of post-modernity. Often used in very different contexts, the term designates the emergence of a complex of new factors which, widespread and powerful as they are, have shown themselves able to produce important and lasting changes. The term was first used with reference to aesthetic, social and technological phenomena. It was then transposed into the philosophical field, but has remained somewhat ambiguous, both because judgment on what is called postmodern is sometimes positive and sometimes negative, and because there is as yet no consensus on the delicate question of the demarcation of the different historical periods. One thing, however, is certain:

the currents of thought which claim to be postmodern merit
appropriate attention ... But we must get beyond destructive
critique of every certitude ... even when it is justified by the
terrible problem of evil. (*FR* 91)

In *FR* 93, Pope John Paul II offers an orientation for a recovery of
tradition which negotiates between modernity and postmodernity
and transcends both perspectives in the light of Christian faith. He
writes of the prime commitment of theology to the understanding
of God's *kenosis*. This itself establishes a way of speaking of God, of
listening to scripture and tradition. It is a context or horizon within
which to integrate reason and faith, but requires rethinking established ways of God-talk and God-theology that rely strongly on
metaphysical foundations. Earlier, in *FR* 23, the pope had written
of the meeting of reason and faith beneath the sign of the wisdom
of the cross. "The depth of revealed wisdom," the letter says, "dis-
rupts the cycle of our habitual patterns of thought." In face of the
wisdom made known on the cross, both human reason and religious
systems have to submit themselves to judgment.

The papal reference is to 1 Corinthians 2, but it could well include the Pauline text for the thirteenth Sunday of the lectionary in
its reference to Christ's willing self-impoverishment. What the pope
underlines is that human reason "finds it inconceivable that suffering and death can express a love which gives itself and seeks nothing
in return" (*FR* 93). Only in this faith may we grasp how reason's
capacity can be properly pursued, and the limits brought to light by
postmodernity's questions given due place, without squandering a
hope that is grounded ultimately in divine love.

The scriptural texts of the Sunday liturgy in question offer a remarkable divine response to those who live in the swing between
the modern and the postmodern. Those who have had these issues
raised for them by the three news items recorded above now hear
stories which proclaim Jesus Christ to be the Lord of life and death,
the Savior from whom the gift of human life comes. Through faith
in him, the Christian community finds the true answer to questions
of life and death, as well as the true ground of hope when sickness, death, and human limits impose themselves on persons and
societies.

In the sequence of readings in the Mass, the attitudes to life and
death of the congregation have first been challenged by the excerpt

from the Book of Wisdom. The ultimate death is the death of the Spirit, the exclusion from the love and providence of God, the loss of eternal communion with God and all the blessed. Whatever else is achieved by way of bettering human life, and this indeed can be done, is put in perspective by the hope of what is eternal. The two Gospel stories then point to Christ himself as the revelation of such wisdom. It is from him that the woman gets healing and through him that the daughter of Jairus is given life.

These gifts are put in perspective by two items in the story that refer to the Gospel of Mark as a whole. First, the works of Jesus are witnessed by Peter, James, and John, who are to be the privileged witnesses of the mystery of his death and resurrection. It is into the proclamation of this mystery that they will have to insert such Gospel narratives as these. Second, when Jesus bids Jairus and his household not to broadcast news of these deeds, it is so that they may not be told out of context. Only those who know the true nature of his messianic mission by reason of their faith in the predictions which he makes throughout this Gospel of his suffering, death, and resurrection can possibly grasp the sense of the works of healing which he performs. They certainly have an immediate purpose of compassionate intervention in aiding those who suffer. Ultimately, however, they are to point to the power of life, and the power over death, which remains unbound at that moment when Jesus in his suffering is subject to the power of the evil one. Whatever the power over the inevitability of suffering and death in our human society, they will never be eliminated, for humankind is ever mortal and sin still stalks and undoes much of what is potential good. Our values and our compassion toward one another and toward the suffering arise most truly from our faith in the power and love of the Crucified One.

The reading from Paul but underlines this truth and gives an almost mundane example of how it affects the way people relate. His appeal for motivation is to the *kenosis* of Christ. His request is that the Church of Corinth in whatever wealth it possesses will come to the aid of other churches that have fewer human resources. To congregations gathered in an affluent society on this Sunday, this says that all the human ingenuity to which they are party is to be put to the service first and foremost of those who suffer and that Americans and Europeans are called upon to break through the boundaries of their own world. They are to go to the aid of other peoples, in ways that take them as fellows and in ways that respect their human dignity. Only in Christ may all Christians face together the enigma of death in its many forms, while drawing on the power to enhance life even in this world that the gifts of intelligence and wisdom give to humans.

Feminist Response

The social, cultural, and ecclesiastical context of our day is marked by the concerns of women, in what are called both feminist and womanist perceptions of human life and of religion itself. These concerns and movements originated on the continents of the north, but they have found place now on other continents and are even given a world stage in the UN-sponsored Women's Conferences. Within the month preceding this Sunday, there was ample news of the Worldwide Women's Meeting at the UNO headquarters in New York.

There is no reason to rehearse the concerns and agenda of these movements at great length since they are well known, even where they are not kindly received or honored. The lens through which the scriptures are read is well described by Elizabeth Johnson:

> The lens of women's flourishing focuses faith's search for understanding in feminist theology. It does so in the context of myriad sufferings resulting from women's being demeaned in theory and in practice in contradiction to the creative power, dignity, and goodness that women appreciate to be intrinsic to their own human identity. When the suffering is brought to consciousness, when its causes are analyzed, when danger-ous and therefore suppressed memories of women's agency are brought to light, and the praxis of resistance and hope are begun, then conditions exist for a new interpretation of the tradition.[4]

In her book *In Memory of Her*, Elisabeth Schüssler Fiorenza gives us a feminist reading of today's Gospel text.[5] She also frequently

---

4. Elizabeth Johnson, *She Who Is: The Mystery of God in Feminist Theological Discourse* (New York: Crossroad, 1992), 18.

5. Elisabeth Schüssler Fiorenza, *In Memory of Her: A Feminist Theological Reconstruction of Christian Origins* (New York: Crossroad, 1984), 124.

appeals to a feminist wisdom which draws on wisdom literature and on the image of Jesus as the Wisdom or Sophia of God.[6]

Schüssler Fiorenza asks the question about what this Gospel story says to the place of woman in society and in the community of discipleship. While even this story may be marked by a patriarchal reading, she points out that in the woman's time an incurably ill person—and this would include a woman suffering the "flow of blood"—would have suffered a double burden. First, she would have been economically impoverished by her quest for a cure, and as a woman she would have had fewer resources. Second, she would have been considered unclean and marginal to the holy people of Israel because of what was looked upon as pollution. While this woman was particularly afflicted, this was a time in which women's blood flow, even during menstruation, made them unclean and in need of ritual purification. This allows the author to connect the story of the young girl to that of the older woman. This girl too would belong to a society which held women to their place and surrounded them with various laws of uncleanness and purification. Both women, the old and the young, are restored to life by Jesus. In his action, he not only shows compassion for the illness but also exhibits his usual attitude, evidenced elsewhere in the Gospel, to the ritual bonds imposed by scribal legalism, in ways quite contrary to the love and wisdom of the God of the covenant.

Within this Gospel narrative, the image of Jesus as the child and embodiment of divine Sophia, or of the Sophia God, stands out with clarity. In his preaching of the reign of God and his gathering of a community of disciples, women were given a new and distinctive place. The reading from the Book of Wisdom is backdrop to this interpretation. The image of God's wholesome concern for creation, for the poor, and for the integrity of human life, as well as the image of the just, found in wisdom literature is important to the understanding of the preaching, deeds, betrayal, and suffering of Jesus. As the author of *In Memory of Her* puts it, "the Palestinian Jesus movement understands the ministry of and mission of Jesus as that of the prophet and child of Sophia sent to announce that God is the God of the poor and heavy laden, of the outcasts and those who suffer injustice."[7] In turn, Paul's admonition that the Christian

---

6. For example, Johnson, *She Who Is*, 87–94, 150–69.
7. Schüssler Fiorenza, *In Memory of Her*, 135.

community should hold the poor, hungry, and suffering in mind, after the fashion of Christ's own self-emptying, seals as it were such a hearing and reception of the Gospel.

Especially on other continents, it may well be to the story of AIDS that a congregation imbued with feminist and womanist concerns is drawn by this day's scriptural proclamation. In the tragedy of this epidemic, women and children are particularly afflicted. In poor societies, they are still those with fewest resources and with the least power in society. In many parts of the world, patriarchy reigns to such an extent, and man's power over women is such, that women are infected by men who have several sexual partners and who have little regard for the possible harm that they may cause to their women folk. Children are born HIV-infected, and millions are left orphans because of the ravage wrought by the epidemic. Not only does the available medication need to be distributed, but human attitudes to women and children need to change, and sexual behavior has to be informed by education, in order to confront the bleak realities. The "collection" for the churches and for the poor from Christian communities who hear this liturgy and partake in its commemoration of Christ takes a variety of shapes. Not only is the contribution of money, always vital, needed, but the uses of political, educational, and commercial resources need channeling.

The ritual behavior of the eucharistic community reflects its own attitudes to women, to the socially different, and to the poor. Communities of hospitality are those that best receive the Gospel's message, those who can ritually express the sense of Jesus' washing of the feet, or the admission to his table of the outcast. Further, if the congregation is to be made attentive to what Jesus and his movement mean to women, rituals and the language of inclusion are called for.

A final caveat is needed before bringing this contextual reading to a conclusion. A hearing of the Gospel and a celebration of the liturgy that take the interests of women seriously are not just "another" context, reading, or interpretation. This is at the core today of how the Gospel is received and preached and of the Church's witness in society. It is matter of grave importance to society, culture, and Church universally. It has to be present in some way in every place and situation. The particularities of the issue are of course different from place to place, but universally today the Christian churches have to integrate women's reception of biblical and liturgical texts into their interpretation, preaching, and celebration.

Response in the Light of Cultural Heritage

While this is still about context, the connection between culture, scripture, and liturgy is worth particular attention. This will be given through two specific examples, namely, the Philippines and contemporary Ireland.

The Church of the Philippines

In 1999, the bishops of the Philippines published a pastoral exhortation about the inculturation of the Gospel and the new evangelization at the advent of a new millennium.[8] It was their intent to place the preaching of the Gospel in the current social and cultural milieus of Filipino peoples, in a time of globalization, to point to the gains and the losses, and to recall traditional values.

The letter is in great part inspired by what Pope John Paul II has said about the inculturation of the Gospel across the world, with reference to cultural diversity. On several occasions Pope John Paul II has addressed the relation of the Gospel and the mystery of Christ to cultures. This he does in face of two realities. The first is the emerging culture of the age on the cusp between the modern and the postmodern, as discussed above. The second is the challenge put to the Church to relate the Gospel to the cultures of new nations, cultures which it often neglected in the past. This is sometimes expressed as the task of inculturation. Both efforts are complicated by the development of new modes of communication that are so massive, inventive, and global and that have an impact on all continents and on all societies.

The pithy phrase which sums up the encounter with cultures is that the Gospel must needs take root in a culture and the culture enriches the Gospel. Obviously this has implications for the ways in which the Gospel is interpreted and made a living part of personal, social, and cultural life. The bishops of the Philippines are concerned with the language of inculturation and with the need for

---

8. National Conference of the Philippines, "Pastoral Letter," 25 January 1999, *Weltkirche* 2 (1999): 43–54.

contextualization in order to take socioeconomic and political conditions into account in the work of a new evangelization. They also
write of basic Christian communities, with their programs of apostolic work, as a locus of privileged attention in the development of
the local church.

In their letter, the bishops of the Philippines take note of how Filipino peoples have in the past integrated many of their traditional
cultural values into their way of living the Gospel. These have to do
with such things as the veneration shown ancestors, respect for the
elderly, adherence to membership of extended families, and hospitality toward strangers. These values also have to do with respect
for the earth and natural forces and the sense of the awesomely
holy in cosmic reality. In religious practice, popular religiosity and
devotions, especially to Christ, Mary, the saints, and remembrance
of the dead, have done much to allow the Gospel to take root in
their cultures.

On the other hand, the bishops note that Church life is too
often lived on a societal or institutional level, with insufficient
involvement of the faithful in building up the Church and the kingdom of God in their environment. Through contact with Western
perspectives, practices, and development, some countervalues have
emerged. These have to do especially with social, political, and family life. In this way, the traditions of the past are now threatened by
a modern secularization.

To offer a Gospel response, the letter takes the model of the
Incarnation of the Word, in Jesus Christ and then in cultures, which
is found in the Second Vatican Council's decree on mission, *Ad
Gentes*.[9] The letter also gives some endorsement to the language
of contextualization used by some Filipino theologians today. With
sharper reference to socioeconomic and political conditions, this
serves to complete the vocabulary of inculturation and the model of
incarnation. Jesus Christ takes form, in his Church, among people
of diverse cultural traditions and always in a living context of total
reality.

The mystery of the cross and resurrection of Jesus Christ is presented as a judgment on what is sinful in society and in Christian
life. In particular this is invoked against the countervalues that too

---

9. Second Vatican Council, Decree on the Church's Missionary Activity, *Ad
Gentes*.

often prevail in Filipino society today, with the breakdown of public service and respect for traditions and the dissolution of families. Rather than look explicitly to the suffering of Christ as evidence of his solidarity with human suffering, as some Third World theologians do, the bishops see the story of this suffering, the resurrection of Christ from the dead, and the anticipation of the second coming as a judgment on human sin and its pollution of life at every level. This does not of course exclude the former perception, but the choice to advance this particular interpretation of the Christ story demonstrates the desire of the Filipino bishops to call their people to conversion in an awareness of having strayed from the way of discipleship.

What then would be the possible response to the readings of the thirteenth Sunday of the liturgical year? The Gospel of the day calls prevailing attitudes to illness and death into question. It asks about the place of the suffering and oppressed in society. Do Filipino peoples, who in the past have found their care for the elderly and the sick confirmed by the Gospel, still live by these values? Or have they gone the way of placing the old and sick outside the domain of the family, either neglecting them or placing their care into the hands of institutions and depriving them of the comforts of living among kin?

The Book of Wisdom resonates readily with the traditional Filipino life, as lived in rural areas. This was marked by attention to the land, reverence for the land, fostering enlarged kinship circles, and a strong sense of the divine providence which attends suffering and ultimately the passage of life and death. One may not expect all connected practices to survive urbanization and the breakup of much of village life, but it may happen that the old values are too quickly abandoned through the adoption of a new lifestyle and a new set of values. In this sense, both the recall to a life of simplicity and trust of the Book of Wisdom and Paul's image of Christ's self-impoverishment may endorse the judgment which the bishops pronounce in their reading of the mystery of the Pasch.

In the eucharistic liturgy, the way of bringing forth and treating the bread and wine may well serve to recall the traditional attitudes to earth, to life passage, and to family life.[10] In the eucharistic prayer, the eschatological expectation of every celebration connects

---

10. This of course becomes harder to do so long as ecclesiastical authorities refuse

with the sense of eschatological judgment that inheres to the interpretation of the Pasch given in the bishops' pastoral letter. The invocation of the Spirit on the Church and on the world would need to be extended to include a wider and more immediate set of petitions. These would affect the current needs of Filipino society and peoples, in ways that draw inspiration from the attention to the immediate found in the prayers of intercession in such ancient anaphoras as that of Basil of Caesarea and the Alexandrian liturgy of Mark.

The Celtic Retrieval in Contemporary Ireland

Talk of the Celtic Tiger is frequent today in light of the Republic of Ireland's emergence in the last two decades from a state of relative poverty. The situation there now is one of a new economic progress, with which goes greater urbanization and a move from the land and from an agricultural economy. While, however, many prosper, political life is corroded by opportunism and the pursuit of even illegal enrichment. With all the progress that has been made, there are the poor who are left behind and there is considerable social chaos in the forms of drug dealing, violence, increased rates of suicide among the young, and the spread of AIDS, mostly associated with drug addiction. The Church too has been revealed in its increasing vulnerability, due to the charges of abuse leveled against clergy and religious and Catholic educational establishments. Some of this is scapegoating, but there is enough substance to the charges to make a Catholic blush and the clergy hide their heads. Bishops too in some cases have been revealed as venal, sometimes proud and unyielding, but mostly as inept in their pastoral charge to guide the faithful through times of transition. Hence Ireland is now a society marked by the Catholic Church's loss of influence and of credibility and the dissolution of Catholic myth and ethos, which leave a moral and spiritual void.

Any community that wishes to face the new situation in the light of Christ looks for the discovery of an alternate spiritual outlook that may inspire the people, while still drawing on ancient traditions. The Gospel is read to a people among whom there is an awakened interest in the old Celtic, even pre-Christian, heritage,

---

to budge on the cultural employ of materials other than wheat and vine in the making of the eucharistic elements.

to which is wedded the desire to answer also to the contribution of Norman and Anglo-Irish traditions that came later.[11] In other words, the attention to Celtic heritage is not an effort to regain a mystical and mythical view of an ancient heritage to be now relived. It is more a matter of drawing resources from a broken tradition in order to forge a new way of life that is more spiritual and less material.

There is new attention, in poetry, prose, and popular music, to the Celtic heritage of communion with earth and with the past, with the living and the dead, in the bonding of a common inheritance, in the memory of its noble ancestors and heroes. To this corresponds the image of Christ as the "king of Friday's people," present in every heart and tongue. Much inspiration is drawn from the Lorica, or Breastplate, of Patrick. Those who want insight into the early days of Christianity in Ireland look to such materials as the Stowe Missal; commentaries on the psalms; devotions to Christ, Mary, and the saints; and penitential practices. In martyrologies and in the canon of the Stowe, there is marked veneration of Old Testament figures and of Irish saints. These present heroic figures of persons, men and women, who endured much as prophets of the true God and who manifest in their stories a forceful sense of the holy present in nature and in natural phenomena. There is ground in such memories for the remembrance of Christ the King, who in his heroic protection and service of his people outdid all heroes in what he endured and in what he gained, even if this meant the giving of his own life.

Gathered for liturgy on the thirteenth Sunday of the year 2000, an Irish congregation would certainly have been alerted during the week to the news items about the decoding of the human genome and about AIDS. They might well now feel themselves as a European people party to the whole range of medical and scientific achievements that constitute the fuller context of the discoveries about human DNA. There is no reason why they too may not be beneficiaries of what this holds in store for the future. On the other hand, recent press stories about AIDS in Ireland itself, about drug addiction, about drug dealing, and about high-level political cor-

---

11. Drawing on many other writings, this author has tried to summarize the contribution to the living of the Gospel that might come from the Celtic heritage. See David N. Power, "Affirmed from Under: Celtic Liturgy and Spirituality," *Studia Liturgica* 27 (1997): 1–32.

ruption are ample cause for postmodern suspicion about both past and future.

In terms of their actuality for an Irish congregation, may the scriptures of the day offer any foundation for the peculiarly Celtic remembrance of the heroic persons of the past who sustained the people in times of lesser fortune? May they give some ground to the remembrance of a heroic Christ who leads by suffering and dying for his people in heroic combat against forces of evil? May they keep alive a sense of old values pertaining to communion with the earth and communities built on generous love, even as the nation prospers? These may well be the questions and issues which such a congregation brings to the day's liturgy. In this regard, Mark's image of Christ as Son of Man and suffering Messiah is still pertinent. His restoration to life of both the older and the younger woman speaks to the values that inject true human and Christian progress. So does Paul's admonition and the remembrance of a simpler past, grounded in a belief in an ever-present divine providence, evoked by the excerpt from Wisdom. One is reminded readily of the words of the Irish poet Seamus Heaney about the world of his childhood, to whose struggles he gladly bids adieu but for whose wonders he yearns:

> I would say that the more important Catholic thing is the ac-
> tual sense of the eternal values and infamous vices which our
> education or formation gives us. There is a sense of profound-
> ness, a sense that the universe is ashimmer with something,
> and Catholicism . . . was the backdrop to the whole thing. The
> world I grew up in offered me a sense that I was a citizen of
> the empyrean—the crystalline elsewhere of the world. But I
> think that's gone from Catholicism now.[12]

Is it ineluctably gone? May it be gathered in, and transformed as context requires, in the Ireland that is in the making? The Gospel issues of the day's liturgy are attitudes to life and death, faith in Christ in face of these realities, and service of the neighbor after the image of Christ who gives himself for us and to us. Fidelity to this Word may well find context among a people who, leaving behind the servitude and drudgery of too many centuries, can now be awakened to richer parts of their inheritance. There was a life of

---

12. Interview with Seamus Heaney, *Irish American* (May-June 1996): 28.

the Spirit that was never subdued in times of adversity but which unhappily risks succumbing to prosperity.

Conclusion

Pursuing the notion of the evolving and even changing life of a text within the life and liturgical practices of a community, this chapter has considered the relation of texts and the prayer which they inspire to specific social and cultural situations. In this way, it was hoped to illustrate an important factor in the interpretation and appropriation of the Word of God in the liturgy.

Part Two

Of Scriptures, Prayers, and Root Metaphors

Chapter Five

Memorial, Memory, and Biblical Imagery

T HE FINE TEST of the truth of interpretation lies in the passage from proclamation to action. The scriptural truth, however, is mediated through ritual and prayer. This is the way in which it leaves its mark on minds and bodies and brings congregations into an encounter with God, through a living participation in the mystery of Jesus Christ. In the process, the "Spirit teaches us how we ought to pray," how to continue to keep alive the memory of this mystery, across time and culture. Without adequate prayer, the Gospel will not take root in a culture. The memorial of Christ has to be couched in the types of prayer in which peoples may recognize their cultural heritage and themselves, this now providing the seedbed in which he takes on new form and presence. It is in their prayer and rites that they refresh their traditions with what they hear in the scriptures.

Liturgy is called both memorial and memory. It is memorial because it is indeed the living presence of Christ's mystery in the midst of his Church. It is called memory to underscore that the memory of Jesus Christ and his deeds is forged through the art of the Church in developing and celebrating rituals and prayers. Memory and memorial are intertwined in a way that defies any purely institutional approach to liturgy. In this chapter, I want to explore what happens to memorial when memory breaks down, and what happens to our reading of the scriptures and their conjunction with liturgical prayer.

If the scriptures are at the heart of celebration, it is nonetheless difficult to explain exactly how they are worked into rite and prayer, being their true foundation even as they merge with more culturally rooted kinds of expression. Context and response bring it about that the process changes according to time and place. It is next to impossible to lay down precise rules as to how this is to be done. When the Constitution on the Liturgy of the Second Vatican Council states that all liturgical development has to be in organic continuity with the past, this is simply to say that we need to be guided by the inspiration of our forebears in the faith. Insight into what they have done, in diverse liturgical traditions, draws forth the present time's energy and creativity. In the process, people's own lives and memories are brought into Christ's memory, carried as it were by the power of language. One might say that the scriptural images, stories, wisdom, prophecy, and hymns are asked to express both the memory of Christ and the living memory of those congregated.

Three things need consideration on this score. First, it is helpful to take a few examples of how the process of integrating scriptures into liturgical prayer has worked in the past, though this can be done quite briefly. Second, it is remarked how in the Roman Rite a prevailing scriptural and cultural paradigm has suffered fissures in recent decades. Third, and most important, we will need to think about the whole problem of remembering the past in our contemporary era and what this means for praying with the scriptures.

Some Liturgical Examples

There are cases when the scriptures of the Mass or other liturgies provide images and metaphors that are integrated into the prayer texts. With the reform of the Roman Rite, we are all familiar with the place in the preface of the eucharistic prayer given to the stories of the Samaritan woman at the Well of Jacob, of the healing of the man born blind, and of the raising of Lazarus. In the blessing of the water for baptism in the current ritual, the waters of creation, the crossing of the Red Sea, the baptism of Jesus in the Jordan, and the Passover of his death and resurrection all provide background for the poetics of the prayer. In this, the Roman Rite now richly draws on Eastern liturgies, whose imagery also occurs in the prayers of other Western churches.[1]

---

1. See the columns which parallel the baptismal blessing in the Catholic liturgy, the Lutheran liturgy, and the Episcopal liturgy, in Philip H. Pfatteicher, *Commentary on the Lutheran Book of Worship: Lutheran Liturgy in Its Ecumenical Context* (Minneapolis: Augsburg, 1990), 42–43.

There are many ancient testimonies to this device. In the Paschal season of the Roman liturgy from early times, the sacrifices of Abel, Abraham, the Passover Lamb, and Melchisedech served not only in scriptural proclamation but also in the eucharistic preface to typify the one sacrifice of Jesus Christ, the true Paschal Lamb. In medieval nuptial blessings for the bride in different traditions, it was assumed that the assembly would be familiar with the stories of the Old Testament women Sarah, Rachel, and Rebecca. To these were added the images found in the passage of Eph 5:22 which compares matrimonial union to the union between Christ and his Church.

What is not so readily grasped, but which is important for the ways in which liturgical families work, is that over a period of time one metaphor provides a dynamic or plot around which the entire liturgy revolves. This is linked with cultural, political, and social realities and provides a way of drawing all reality into the Christian story and into a particular way of presenting the Christian perception of reality. The way in which this is party to historical, social, and cultural factors is important in seeing how language works to proclaim and ensure a living presence of Christ within a people. Some examples may be quickly reviewed.

The anaphora of John Chrysostom became the primary eucharistic prayer of Byzantine liturgy, remaining such through a host of liturgical developments that marked the association between Christian revelation, empire, and the divine glory represented in architecture, art, ritual, and prayer.[2] This anaphora is rightly credited with its contribution to the development of *anamnesis* and the theological concept of the memorial of past events, which is at the same time an eschatological expectation of the future. What, however, exists at the center of this liturgical and theological development is the dominant image of the second part of the anaphora, where the Father is thanked because "you so loved the world that you gave your only-begotten Son that all who believe in him may not perish, but have eternal life." The subsequent marvels of rite and music and iconography, portraying Christ as Pantocrator and Theotokos and High Priest of the heavenly/earthly liturgy, are rooted in this image. In liturgy and other aesthetic forms, under whichever of these titles Christ is represented, it is always the love of the Father in the

---

2. See Hugh Wybrew, *The Orthodox Liturgy* (Crestwood, N.Y.: St. Vladimir's Seminary Press, 1990).

sending of the Son which is at work. This is also given a very local tone in the prayer's intercessions, which include all those who belong, united through the Spirit, in any local church—the saints and patriarchs remembered, the bishop and his clergy, the emperor and the empress, their court and army, those who live in virginity, those who live the heremitical life, city-dwellers and rural-dwellers, travelers, prisoners, and the sick. Between the Christ worshipped in his glory and the ranks of the people from the most noble to the lowest, there is a perfect communion in the Spirit, and every grace emanates from the love of the Father.

The Roman canon, as is well known, made a delicate and keenly woven use of the image of sacrifice to suggest the relation of the Church to God and to Christ, while at the same time taking in the lives, prayers, and gifts of the people. The image has its roots in what Paul says of Christ's death as sacrifice and about the spiritual sacrifices of believers. It is, however, also an image much prone to assimilating elements from various cultural and religious heritages.

In the time of the decline of the empire and its institutions at Rome, under such great pontiffs as Gregory the Great, this served to present the Church in all its ranks and in its liturgy as the divinely appointed new *plebs,* united in one sacrifice before God and resplendent in its almost military glory. When the Roman liturgy crossed the Alps under the Emperor Charlemagne, who had placed the seat of empire in those northern regions, the canon's image and metaphor of sacrifice still provided a unifying vision. It consolidated the empire of Charlemagne in its image of itself as a theocracy, where Church and state composed a harmonious unity. The one sacrifice of Christ celebrated by the Church, whether in a great public building, in a small rural church, in an abbey, or in a private oratory, was the one center around which all could be built. Within itself and within prayer, the image gathers themes of adoration, of expiation, and of reconciliation, which outside and in the liturgy could be realized in a variety of forms and artifices. Later, when empire and Church were less potent, among Christian peoples there grew up a sacrificial spirituality promoting a life of self-sacrifice in communion with Christ, of penance for sin that drew its power from this one sacrifice, of heroic gift of self for the service of God and even of country. Within this unity, and around this central still-point of sacrifice, there was ample room for a proliferation of specific cultural realizations and people-centered acts of devotion.

The variation on the themes worked by Martin Luther in his liturgy of baptism and the Lord's Supper was made possible by the use of other biblical images and metaphors. The death of Christ was no less a sacrifice for Luther than for Rome, and the work of the liturgy was to bring its fruit to the people. However, he wanted nothing of the Church's association with Christ in offering this sacrifice since she was beneficiary, not actor thereof. Around this image of Christ's expiatory sacrifice with its promise of the forgiveness of sins, he wove two other images. The one was that of all Christians as a priestly people, which did away with the idea of the clergy as the special order of priests who could offer Christ's sacrifice. Liturgy and prayer are the work of the people, not of the pope and the priests. On the other hand, to assure that their worship is entirely one of receiving from Christ, Luther brought to the fore the Pauline image of divine justification. It is only by the righteous act of God in overlooking human sin, because of the sacrifice of his Son for sin, that Christians are justified and God himself worshipped and honored. The Flood Prayer which Luther composed for baptism exemplifies his thought and his use of biblical language:

> We yield thee hearty thanks, most merciful Father, that it hath pleased thee to regenerate this infant with thy Holy Spirit, to receive him for thine own Child by adoption, and to incorporate him into thy holy Church. And humbly we beseech thee to grant, that he being dead unto sin, and living unto righteousness, and being buried with Christ in his death, may crucify the old man, and utterly abolish the whole body of sin; and that, as he is made partaker of thy Son, he may also partake of his resurrection; so that with the residue of thy holy Church, he may be an inheritor of thine everlasting kingdom, through Christ our Lord. Amen.[3]

Breakdown of the Scriptural Paradigm of Sacrifice

Many among us are glad to have the Roman liturgy celebrated in the vernacular. Of singular importance are the possibility of hearing the scriptures in one's own language and the way in which this

---

3. In J. D. C. Fisher, *Christian Initiation: The Reformation Period* (London: SPCK, Alcuin Club, 1970), 11.

has opened up avenues to a better knowledge of the Word of God. Active participation, with diverse ministries assumed by all the baptized and not solely by clerics, is also widely considered a boon. Yet we remain vaguely ill at ease with our renewed liturgy. The more critical speak of reforming the reform, or even of reforming the reformers (by which is often meant those deemed expert and knowledgeable in matters liturgical). Rather widely, it is felt that the liturgy is often celebrated in the absence of beauty or even of a modest and basic decorum. Solutions diverge. Some would have the Church return to the use of Latin and Gregorian chant, and would likewise highlight the role of priest and clergy, so as to restore a more hierarchical and sacred feel to the celebration of Christ's mystery. Others would see this as precisely the road not to be traveled.

It is the breakup of the sacrificial and priestly paradigm which is at the heart of the problem the Church faces in restoring a liturgy worthy of the mystery celebrated. What appears most openly is the desire on the part of many to affirm and celebrate the Church of Christ as the Church of the baptized, certainly replete with ordained and other ministries, but not clerically and hierarchically configured. There is with this the hope to express the closeness of Christ to his people in and through the sacramental elements, rather than seeing these kept in some fashion the preserve of the clergy and finding them cut off by sacrosanct rituals. Is it not possible to maintain and represent a sense of the holy that is not dependent on the sacred barrier between clergy and people, hierarchy and faithful?

What needs to be noted is that the central image of sacrifice, not as it originated in the scriptures but as over time it took shape in Roman governance, liturgy, and spirituality, no longer provides the Church in its unity with a paradigm of communion with and in Christ. It was taught and celebrated as a priestly and hierarchical act. It served as cornerstone to a spirituality of penance, retribution, and negation by which people lived in past ages, and indeed unto their own sanctification and God's glory. Persons of genius, especially artists and musicians, could somehow realize their talents within this paradigm without being clergy, having another port of entry into the sacred mystery. Most of the faithful lived subordinately, though often finding an outlet for an affective piety in popular devotions that looked with compassion on Christ's suffering and nurtured instincts of penance and self-sacrifice.

New perceptions of the human, of the interpersonal, and of the order of things make this particular representation of the sacrificial unworkable. Even studies of the origin of the Christian use of sacrificial and priestly imagery question the hold of this medieval Roman rendition. We live for the moment between scattered metaphors, in the crisscross of diverse representations, kept together (if this indeed be so) only (indeed!) by the desire to live in the power and memory of Jesus Christ, however this be formulated afresh over the course of time. Many directives keep coming from the magisterium but do not necessarily take, the exercise of authority not being matched by a comparable rhetoric of language and example.

The one fascinating arrow that has been cast is the accent put on the images of God's own *kenosis* in Christ and on the reconciliation which may come about through a justice grounded in this truth and example. Developed by scriptural scholars and theologians in various Christian churches, this has been sanctioned by no less a person than Pope John Paul II, as seen earlier. While he puts it forward as a challenge to theologians, to the purification of memories, and to those who in high office serve a global society, it is a challenge also to liturgy. Indeed, if it does not take hold there, and there find ritual, rhetorical, and aesthetic representation, it will not form the Christian mind and heart, nor meet the sensitivities of those for whom keeping memory is profoundly painful and bitter.

Unwholesome Memories Made Whole?

We live in an age when remembering has become difficult. That is not only to say that change is so rapid and people are so dedicated to the immediate sound or sight that they pass beyond the effort to remember. This may be true but the deeper challenge comes from the senselessness of much which has taken place in the course of the last century of the passing millennium. Some memories, especially those of the greatest human tragedies, are hard to bear and so tend to be shunned. Some are such that though ingrained in the skin, they defy expression. It is asked whether speaking or writing of them, whether giving them representation in art or in film, is not to disrespect those who suffered and died. In our effort to make sense of things for ourselves, we risk betraying the dead. For religious believers, furthermore, many human memories sit ill with the remembrance of God's covenant or with faith in the resurrection of Christ.

The difficulty of speech that besets us is captured in the lines of
a poem by Paul Celan, "Tübingen, January":

> Should,
> Should a man,
> should a man come into the world today, with
> the shining beard of the
> patriarchs: he could,
> if he spoke of this
> time, he
> could
> only babble and babble
> over, over
> againagain.[4]

Examples of episodes and events in the relatively recent past, to
which it is hard to give expression, include first and foremost the
Holocaust of the Jewish people under the Nazi and fascist regimes.
This is a reality that affects all humanity and in a particular way
Jewish and Christian peoples. Of it, it has been said in the words
of George Steiner, to quote but one writer: "The world of Ausch-
witz lies outside speech as it lies outside reason. To speak of the
unspeakable is to risk the survivance of language as creator and
bearer of humane, rational truth."[5] Yet it is in the very recognition that it is outside rational truth, and indeed that it breaks the
truth of religious story and ritual, that some attempt is made to
express it. This is done in several ways. As ground to all else,
there is the exacting device of gathering testimonies, of allowing
voice to the victims. There is also the taut poetry of one such as
Paul Celan, the disturbing prose of Primo Levi, the film and the
fiction that must ever resist the temptation to rationalize, to sen-
timentalize, and to moralize. In the field of religious expression,
Jewish communities work its remembrance into their Passover Hag-
gadah.[6] For Christians, John Paul II has used the language of prayer

4. *Poems of Paul Celan*, trans. Michael Hamburger (New York: Persea Books,
1995), 181.
5. George Steiner, *Literature and Silence: Essays 1958–1966* (London and
Boston: Faber & Faber, 1985), 146.
6. See the study by Lawrence Hoffman, *Beyond the Text: A Holistic Approach
to Liturgy* (Bloomington: Indiana University Press, 1987), 126–48.

and ritual to take account of the memory of this event, as for example in his Jubilee Year visit to Israel. His words at the Holocaust Memorial and his very presence at the Wailing Wall of the Temple put fire to Christian imagination's complacency in face of this horror.

Other examples of inexpressible memories in our time abound. For the people of the United States of America, the effort is called forth to work Vietnam, Korea, and the Civil War into meaningful memories that must not, however, be banal or ideological. There is also the task of making the memories of African American and native Indian peoples an intrinsic part of the country's history and future. Political discourse, art, literature, and film have never been so challenged.

For the Irish people in their new-found prosperity and European identity, a new awareness has emerged in some circles that the remembrance of the Great Famine of the mid–eighteenth century, with its horrible deaths and consequent emigration, calls for fresh expression, both factual and artistic. It is intrinsic to whatever new national myth points to the future of a society that is more pluralistic and open than that which constituted the early years of the independent state. On the religious front, nothing has ever taken the place of the recitation of the *De Profundis* psalm at the end of every Mass, a practice all too blithely jettisoned with the advent of liturgical reform.

For all African, Asian, and Latin American countries and cultures in this postcolonial era, it has to be asked how their past, in its richness and in its bitter recollection, is to be integral to their political, literary, and religious future. The Church talks of inculturation and contextualization and of integrating a people's religious language and ritual. But if the past and its people are not remembered, not given voice, in this process, there is little truth to it.

Language, in all its forms, is truly strained by the effort to remember. Yet its task is to be honored. In remembering, we are not primarily concerned with the literal facts of the past, with the details of events as they took place. What shapes a community are not the brute facts of history but images of the past embodied in language. With regard to specifically religious remembrance, Lawrence Hoffman has written: "Clearly, one of the prime functions of liturgy is the presentation of sacred myths to sacred assemblies, that through a selective vision of the past, they may learn how to plot the future."[7] The selection of course has to be carefully, if creatively, negotiated, and the Word of the scriptures plays a key role in the exercise.

Language is a complex network of words, signs, images, metaphors, assertions, comparisons, questions and answers, affirmations and negations. It belongs to and in a life. It affects and is affected by political, economic, domestic, and public factors. For a people or in a religious system, there are key stories that identify beliefs and shape the people or the system into a unity. The strategy is to organize all the forms of expression so as to give them a center, as it were, in some root metaphor or set of metaphors. It is through the operation of these metaphors that the plot and direction of memory take shape.

American history and institutions, for example, often appeal to the leitmotif suggested by the Declaration of Independence in its opening words, "We the People." Alternately, they turn to the Bill of Rights, with its claim, "We hold these truths to be self-evident." Such metaphors work, even when it seems they do not work. The puzzle and estrangement of the Vietnam War, for example, could be expressed by saying that it was not "of the people." Neither could it be related by the populace at large to any inalienable truth or right. Even to this day, writers may refer to it as a betrayal of the basic sense of the nation expressed in its foundations.

For his part, Pope John Paul II has put the challenge to the Church of remembering the past through Christian memory and expression. Referring to what has often been allowed to fall into oblivion, he called for the *purification of memories* as a central obligation of the Jubilee Year of 2000 of the common era.[8] The challenge clearly goes beyond that particular year.

The use of root metaphors is built into biblical discourse. There is the constant return of such metaphors as the reign of God, the promised land, the servant of Yahweh, and the Passover. While these images do not have a definitive and irreversible meaning, they have a poetic force or dynamic that serves well in many kinds of literature to express a constant thread of fidelity in God's action, running through a considerable diversity of historical realities. The difficulty

---

7. Ibid., 144.
8. This has been elaborated upon theologically by the International Commission of Theologians in its document *Memory and Reconciliation;* see *Origins* 29, no. 39 (2000): 625–44.

now is to weave these and other metaphors into story and song in such a way that they serve the purification of memories and capture the past in such a way that a vision of a possible future remains. There is precedent on which to draw. In the books of the scriptures, there are many examples in the history of Israel of songs and stories that renew the remembrance of the past and the vision of the future in times of distress and loss. Lamentation, such as that found in Jeremiah or in some of the psalms, has played its part in this. So has apocalyptic imagery and the ability to give fresh account of the people's origins.

The question asked here is about remembering events of the common era, the disasters that affect peoples and nations of different times and places. Do the imagery and the remembrance of our Judeo-Christian scriptures serve us in a time such as this? How the appeal to a scriptural tradition affects the remembering is the key issue for Christian faith and ritual.

To gain some insight into what this involves and of how it may break down, a particular nonliturgical example may help. I will turn then to a particular historical event of a particular people and to the poetic expression that has been offered as a way of retaining hope in face of loss. It will show both how biblical imagery was invoked and how it broke down when new events cast doubt on the vision it projected.

Poetry of the Irish Famine

As an example of how biblical images and stories expressed the stressful experience and memories of a people, we can look at the poetry of the Irish famine of 1845 forward.[9] Biblical images and cultural myth merged in the effort to speak the unspeakable.

While the Irish famine is most bitterly remembered because of the numerous deaths it brought about, it also marked the failure of an agriculture, however poor, on which people had come to rely and the breakdown of a whole way of life. It was followed by political and poetic rhetoric which blamed the British government for its failure to help the people, an explanation which in recent revisionist

---

9. An anthology of the poetry of the famine has been compiled by Chris Morash, ed., *The Hungry Voice: The Poetry of the Irish Famine* (Blackrock, Dublin: Irish Academic Press, 1989).

history allows for much more nuance.[10] In the ways in which it was remembered, it was associated with a mysticism of Gaelic and Celtic culture which was threatened by this event and which patriots, both political and literary, sought to revive as the hope for the future of the country. Despite being a senseless calamity, it was nonetheless woven into a particular myth of heroicity and survival. Now that this myth has broken down, it is possible to discard the famine altogether from living memory, but in truth it is necessary to pass through a more accurate historical account to a new way of speaking that responds, perhaps critically, to present reality, present ways of looking at Irish history, and present ways of building a future.

The most prominent poet of the famine is James Clarence Mangan.[11] To voice sorrow over what befell the people deprived of their staple food and condemned to hunger and death, Mangan turns to the lamentations of Jeremiah over Jerusalem.[12] Of those who pass by, he asks them to "to stop short awhile" and see if earth has ever seen a like sorrow. Pointing to the "dark iniquites" that belied Judea's vaunted faith in God, he does not hesitate to attribute their affliction to the people's sins, but he also lays blame on their enemies. His final vision is one of an apocalyptic reversal when these enemies will be laid low and the Lord will "make vintage of them all." In a poem entitled "A Vision: A.D. 1848,"[13] Mangan describes the event of the famine by following through the scenes of the Book of Revelation, until the end. In the final section of the poem, assigned to the years 1848–50, he beholds in the west "a cloud lurid with gore," approaching shoreward, hears the trumpet, and sees lightning and thunder that presage God's judgement. This leaves him with the question as to what might "next befall" and the wonder of how all might end. It is thus in the throws of this mystery that he awakens from his sleep and his dream so that he cannot say how the catastrophe, in God's judgment, is to end.

As Chris Morash points out in his introduction to this collection of poems, Mangan was not the only one to look to the Book of

---

10. See, for example, Christine Kinealy, *This Great Calamity: The Irish Famine 1845–52* (Dublin: Gill and Macmillan, 1994); Cormac O Gráda, *Ireland: A New Economic History 1780–1939* (Oxford: Oxford University Press, 1994). For an overview of studies in different fields, see Cathal Pórtéir, ed., *The Great Irish Famine* (Cork and Dublin: Mercier Press, 1995).

11. Morash, *Hungry Voice*, 130–59.

12. Ibid., 135–38.

13. Ibid., 146–49.

Revelation for the imagery whereby to construe the famine disaster. Morash finds that this kind of poetry is too wedded to "millenarian" (his spelling) imagery and explanation. It looks for an explanation of the disaster in divine plan and judgment. It supposes that God has himself visited the earth with this plague. It must dub those who failed (for one reason or another) to rescue the people as enemies, who in turn are to be subjected to divine punishment and judgment. In short, while it finds a voice for lamentation and distress, it feeds ancient enmities and in the end wants to ascribe meaning to the senseless, by looking to divine intervention. Morash wonders why these poets could not look elsewhere in the Bible for something that would give a more fitting response:

> The millenarian [*sic*] imagery ... is but one example of the latent apprehension of meaninglessness generating a search for alternative conventions. Instead of turning to the obvious Biblical text with which to encompass the problem of suffering, the Book of Job, or even instead of turning to the passages dealing with suffering in the Gospels, the majority of the famine poets who attempted to work within a Biblical framework drew on what is probably the most imagerially chaotic book in the Bible, the Book of Revelation,[14] as the only Biblical text capable of providing images as extreme and as disorienting as the world around them had suddenly become.[15]

While there is no direct line to follow from one to the other, the poetry of revolution which fed the armed insurrection against British rule, and the myth of the early Irish state after 1921, showed the same intent to find meaning in suffering, and to find it in evocations of God's design as shown in Christ. Padraig Pearse wrote a poetry which is said to have inspired a "messianism and a sacrificial cult of violence as a rationale for political insurrection."[16] It is not of course that Pearse is wrong in finding the motif in the Gospel that "out of death comes life and out of death victory," but

---

14. Obviously, on this book one would need to look at recent scholarship to do it justice. Morash is primarily concerned with how it was read and used in this famine poetry.

15. Morash, *Hungry Voice*, 36–37.

16. Luke Gibbons, "Challenging the Canon: Revisionism and Cultural Criticism," in *The Field Day Anthology of Irish Writing* (Derry: Field Day Publications, 1991), 3:565.

what is challenged is the alliance of this imagery with a particular type of politics and insurrection, thus glorifying blood-sacrifice and violence in the name of Catholicism and a concept of Ireland's destiny. While he and his cause may suffer too severely, both as poet and as patriot, from his contemporary critics, there is no doubt that he related his military plans to a mystic vision of Ireland and the Irish people that was unfolded in Christian and biblical imagery. It is this which is called into question, for the narrow political and moral provincialism which enveloped the early decades of the state, for its failure to do justice to a more subtle historical remembrance, and for its inability to give any tone or future to current experience.

Poetry in the New Ireland

If remembrance of the famine, and indeed of other events of Irish history, cannot be embraced through these past forms of biblical imagery, how may memory survive? It is the sad truth that many people in Ireland today seem to have belatedly espoused all the Enlightenment values without reserve or nuance. This draws the ironic gaze of poets since it is no response to the pitfalls and the closed vision of republican and romantic Celticism. This almost skeptical poetry is much more sober in its appeal to memory and imagination.

Already in 1916, one of the leaders of the insurrection, Thomas MacDonagh, poet and critic, had taken his distance from the Celtic mythology and messianism of Padraig Pearse.[17] For him, revival in fact means allowing for discontinuity with the past. It is no simple matter of recuperation. There was to be no simple recovery of a Gaelic golden age, and yet there was to be some way of moving forward ever through evocation of a broken tradition. Some breakdown is inevitable, some loss of language. In the literature of recent decades this has affected all things Irish, including the ways of speaking of the famine.

There is some tentative use of images and metaphors, conveying impressions and strategies of language rather than a plot into which to insert the narrative. The images are found by digging into memory and even in the landscape of field and sky. In a poem entitled

---

17. Ibid., 3:564–65.

"The Heart of Ireland,"[18] Peter Fallon describes how working in a field evokes memory and causes him to "backtrack" "to the far end of those drills," where one finds "the heart of Ireland" and the stench of the rotting potatoes. This is a challenge to faith, presenting the need to strain against a loss of faith in God and in the future of the country. The poet calls the reader to a newfound faith that may emerge from this trial of memory, but he does not give any images for the form it may take.

For his part, Seamus Heaney in "At a Potato Digging"[19] brings forth how all work in the field is done in the shadow of the famine. Laborers at a potato-digging must find harmony with the earth (and indeed Ireland itself if it is to go forward heedful of its past). The potatoes dug up are themselves reminders of "live skulls, blind-eyed, balanced on wild higgledy skeletons." Workers in the field are tempted to make a god of the famine and to "make a seasonal altar of the sod." However, another way forward is to be sought for the workings of memory, one that offers in human art and creativity a release and a hope.

From another perspective, Eavan Boland's "The Making of an Irish Goddess"[20] gives voice to the memories that inhabit a woman's body, in which there is an inscription of the agonies suffered by mothers who see the agony of their doomed children. The failed harvests and the rotting fields and the doom of their children cast a blight on the hearts of mothers.

Since there is no ready response to such memories, either in Irish tradition and revival, in ancient Druidic religions, or in Christian faith, the language that dares point to a future is tentative. Finding fragments from the past, searching out a language that draws on the imagination of space and place, and on cultural heritage, despite breakdown and discontinuity, is like taking a journey for which the point of arrival is uncertain.[21]

There are some remarkable evocations of this journey, harrowing as it is, in the poetry of Eavan Boland, who is both ready to speak of the Irish famine and at the same time to enfold it into larger

---

18. In *Field Day Anthology*, 3:1417–18.
19. Seamus Heaney, *Death of a Naturalist* (London: Faber and Faber Ltd., 1966), 31–33.
20. Eavan Boland, *Outside History* (Manchester: Carcanet, 1990).
21. See the excerpt from Richard Kearney, "Transitions," in *Field Day Anthology*, 3:631–33.

memories of distress, loss, and rapacious death. In her poem "The Journey,"[22] she is led to behold all the plagues, wars, and famines in which women saw their children "stolen and plunged to death." She draws on a passage from Virgil's *Aeneid,* book VI:

> Immediately cries were heard. These were the loud wailing of infant souls weeping at the very entrance-way; never had they had their share of life's sweetness for the dark day had stolen them from their mothers' breasts and plunged them to a death before their time.

The Anglo-Irish poet tells of her journey into this netherworld of horrors, accompanied by her guide. Seeing there women with their dead children clinging to their shriveled breasts, she begs, "let me be, let me at least be their witness." The reply is significant. Though what has been seen is beyond speech, it is not beyond love. In her very first sight of these women and their children, the poet had indeed been struck by the fact that even in their distress they did yet portray "the grace of love." Only a witness who can see this grace and can herself love, may in any way, however inadequate, be a witness across time and history. This is why she seems to hear the injunction: "you will remember it" and so testify to it.

At the risk of being overanalytical in writing of poetry, one may find certain pointers in this poetry to the travail of memory. First, there must be those who speak and write of these things, who are witnesses to them, lest we all forget. Second, even this witness must acknowledge how much what is witnessed is "beyond speech, beyond song." Third, it is not "beyond love." What has been witnessed carries within itself, despite the horror of the vision, "the grace of love," and only a loving vision may express its memory.

There is not much biblical resonance in this new poetry, but it is not, for all that, unbiblical. Though seldom explicitly religious, it brings its own insights to a religious quest. How such poetic sentiment may merge with a specific Christian memory through the force of language is a challenge to oral and written forms of Christian expression. For Irish people, it asks what takes the place of the *De Profundis* at the end of Mass.

---

22. In *Field Day Anthology,* 3:1396–98.

The Roman Liturgy Revisited

Pointers to the Use of Scriptures and Biblical Images

This detour into the poetic evocation of the memory of the Irish famine gives us pointers to what to make of the use of scriptures and biblical images in the Roman liturgy. First, this liturgy has been richly biblical from the beginning, but it has always wedded the scriptures with cultural imagery and idiom, thus making it capable of speaking to passing realities of time and place. Second, as it imbedded itself into the consciousness of the medieval and post-Tridentine Church, the evocation of the scriptural matrix is dominated by the language of sacrifice and by a particular liturgical practice that made of it a singularly hierarchical activity and a rather harsh metaphor of retribution and penance. Third, this has to a great extent broken down in face of contemporary Western culture, as it is also incapable in its Western form of speaking to the postcolonial worlds of other Christianities. Fourth, as we are globally confronted with harsh, unspeakable memories, for which the Irish famine may here serve as metaphor, the inadequacy of the later Roman appropriation of the language of sacrifice confronts us. Fifth, the language of prayer and the integration of scriptural recollection into prayer as prayed, and not simply as text, are tentative: they constitute a journey that imposes itself upon the Church. Sixth, this journey must bear witness and let the past give its witness. Seventh, in the motif suggested by Pope John Paul II for Jubilee 2000, it has to embrace the purification of memories in such ways that the Church sees herself judged in order to be purified. Eighth, some use of image and metaphor is emerging but cannot be readily reduced to a pattern with clear weavings and boundaries.

Illustrating these points can be done economically in two steps. The first will be to consider the creative heritage of the Roman liturgy. The second will be pursued in the next chapter, with an inquiry about the evolving use of root metaphors.

Creativity of the Roman Liturgy

The best way to crack open the tradition of the Roman liturgy, to reveal its rich heritage, is to consider its original creativity. It is on the very basis of this creativity that we may find the possibilities of a different appropriation and even of new compositions. We will look at both the composition and content of a sample choice of texts from its prayers. This may be of service not only to Catholics but to other churches, not only for the West but for all peoples to whom liturgies first came in Western garb and who are now creatively drawing on other heritages.

The Roman Canon of the Mass

The form of address of the canon is derived from the address of petition to the emperor or one of his representatives. As a rhetorician or suppliant might affirm the majesty and governance of the imperial power, so the canon affirms the majesty and governance of God. As a Roman suppliant would see a clear, ordered structure to the rule of the state and its colonies, so the prayer sees creation and redemption to be ordered according to the dispositions of divine providence. The prayer is written primarily in the form of supplication, the petition for a hearing being motivated by appeal to benevolence and order. The approach to the sovereign is through the offering of sacrifice, and so too the canon is couched in the terms of such an offering.

The employment of the language and metaphors of sacrifice, with its rich Latin vocabulary of gift, office, and sacrificial action, is the hallmark of the canon's creativity. Though it is proclaimed by the presider, it is by no means a dominantly hierarchical prayer. Rather, it is the prayer of all the people, their sacrifice. Through the use of the language of sacrifice, with its many rich terms, the prayer embraces the prayer of the people, their bringing of gifts, and their very lives. At this point, the New Testament transposition from ritual sacrifice to the prayer and action of the Christian people converges with the Roman instinct to seek favor through sacrifice.

In the canon, this same language of sacrifice, gift, and offering is a happy and striking way of including the memory of Christ's death and resurrection, the history of the Old Testament, the action of Christ at the Last Supper, and the relation of the Church to the heavenly liturgy. That the action begins and culminates in God's condescension and redemptive love appears from a comparison between the canon and the language of exchange or *commercium* found in other prayers for the Mass that belong to the early compositions of this rite. As a prayer over the gifts for Christmas has it,[23]

---

23. For example, the prayer over the gifts for a Christmas Mass: "May the offering of this day's feast be pleasing to you, O Lord, so that with the pouring out of your

the exchange of gifts originates not with the Church but with God's creation. When this remains the order of redemption and not only of creation, the initiative of all that is celebrated in the eucharistic memorial lies in the Incarnation, where the Son exchanged his divine nature for human. In this way, though the language of the Mass is that of rites of sacrifice, what marks in effect the Christian dispensation of sacrifice is that it originates in God's love and that expiatory rite is replaced by Christian action and prayers of praise and supplication. The gift exchange inherent to what is now called sacrifice begins in the taking on of human nature on the part of the Son. Such enrichment of humanity transforms human nature, its orientation, and all its actions, including its ritual behavior.

The Roman Collects

The current English translation of the Roman Sacramentary reveals some trouble in finding a suitable name for the first presidential prayer to be said by the priest. Here it will be called by its traditional name, the collect. The collects which can be dated back to the history of liturgical composition in the Church in Rome show creativity both in form and in content.

The principles of liturgical change are related by the documents of the magisterium, beginning with the Constitution on the Liturgy of the Second Vatican Council, to a model of organic development. It is said that any changes made need to be in organic continuity[24] with the past of the tradition and must respect the substantial unity of the Roman Rite,[25] as kept from its beginnings and down through its history. What these terms mean is not crystal clear, and both of them need to be pondered and understood in light of historical origins and change over the course of time.

The substance, or substantial unity, of the Roman Rite is a metaphor for what remains the same even in the course of modification so that an identity of the rite across time may be affirmed. If related to its appearances, as the substantial has to be in order to be known, it is clear that it does not primarily mean a given set of texts or ritual actions. A good comparison is with the human body of any

---

grace, we may through this sacred exchange be found in the form of him in whom our nature abides with you." The translation is my own. Original in the Verona Sacramentary, no. 1249.

24. Second Vatican Council, *Constitution on the Sacred Liturgy*, no. 23.

25. Ibid., no. 38.

person, which changes considerably in appearance and in what it can physically manage over the course of the years. Whatever these changes, and modern medical techniques make it possible even to remove and introduce new organs, the person remains the same. This is, however, not a purely physical observation. Consciousness, memory, goals, and ideals, in tandem with bodily change, constitute the reality of the person. Hence in talking of the organic unity and continuity of the Roman Rite, we have to ask not only what remains the same in appearance and what has changed, but we must look for insight into how these changes were brought about, what dynamic of spirit and action influenced them. This can be related to the second metaphor, organic continuity, since what is noted is the organic workings of the rite as the rite of peoples, not simply as a set of rituals and texts. It is only in the light of such insight that it is possible to talk seriously of organic continuity and substantial unity. The more particular interest in these lines is to know what this means by way of relating scripture to life and vice versa.

Looking at the prayer of the Roman Rite called the collect offers some such insights. In a careful analytical study of Roman collects in the present sacramentary[26] which have early origins, Gerard Moore, following the most influential authors in this field, notes that the Roman Latin prayers have roots in Roman pagan prayer. In style, they have a typical Roman character and appeal, but they are enriched and transformed by a vocabulary assumed from Latin translations of the Bible. He quotes the noted Latinist Christine Mohrmann:

> In the close-knit, well-composed phrases of the Roman orations, in which the collect resumes, as it were, the prayer of the faithful, we find traces of the style processes of the art of polished speech, taught and practiced in the schools of Rome.[27]

By looking at concrete examples, Moore also demonstrates how creative these prayers are in content. They can respect the approach to majesty of the Roman tradition even while embracing scriptural idioms of divine and human action. They can be open and univer-

---

26. Gerard Moore, *Vatican II and the Collects for Ordinary Time: A Study in the Roman Missal (1975)* (San Francisco: International Scholars Publications, 1998).
27. Ibid., 16.

sal in their petition even while responding directly to the concrete events and realities of Rome and the Roman Church.

One fine example is taken from the collect prescribed for the fourth Sunday in ordinary time.[28] The following is as close a translation as possible:

> Grant to us, Lord God, to worship you with all our mind and to love all people with spiritual affection.[29]

This prayer is first found in the old Roman collection called the Verona Sacramentary, and is a composition by the pope, Gelasius I. It was written by him in the hope that by a just liturgical celebration he might counter the participation of Christians in the Roman festival of Lupercalia marking mid-February and the proximity of spring. These were celebrations of erotic love and fertility. They venerated the gods of the underworld and included erotic and at times cruel rites. To take part in such festivities was, for Christians, to run counter to the true worship of God revealed in Jesus Christ, as well as to the love of God and neighbor taught in the Old and New Testaments. The language of the prayer is both succinct and pointed. Its appreciation requires some admiration of Latin style. In one taut sentence, the petition of the prayer is that Christians might worship the God of Christianity *tota mente*, that is, totally and with undivided minds and hearts. On this there must follow the love of neighbor which is marked by a *rationabilis affectus*, that is, a spiritual, not carnal, affection. The use of the Latin translation of biblical texts is apparent. *Tota mente* derives from the great commandment of love in Deut 6:4–6. *Rationabilis* translates terms for Christian dispositions of love in such texts as Psalm 118 and 1 Pet 1:22ff.:

> Now that you have purified yourselves by obedience to the truth until you feel sincere affection toward your fellow Christians, love one another wholeheartedly with all your strength. You have been born again, not of mortal but of immortal parentage, through the living and enduring word of God.

Both what the prayer seeks to counter and what it proposes as

---

28. Ibid., 99.
29. The translations used for the collects are those worked out by Moore, with this author's guidance.

the virtue of Christian life and worship may well indeed escape the attention of an American congregation. The erudition in things Roman which it supposes, and which allows for a true admiration of the prayer, cannot and should not be assumed in congregations of other places and cultures. In those creative writers, however, who can contribute to public prayer, it is a profound inspiration.

Another example, now found in the Missal for the twenty-third Sunday of ordinary time, originates in another Roman collection of texts, usually called the Gelasian in today's studies of liturgies.[30] In English translation, this reads:

> God, through whom redemption comes for us
> and adoption is bestowed upon us,
> look favorably upon the children of your love,
> so that to those who believe in Christ,
> true freedom and eternal inheritance may be granted.

In all probability, this was a prayer to be used not for the Mass but for the public, nonmonastic celebration of an hour of the Office in Paschaltide. Its creativity is found in the way that it can accommodate the classical style of prayer to the vocabulary of the Latin translation of the Letter to the Galatians. This is in fact the vocabulary which it uses to celebrate the mystery of redemption as celebrated in the Paschal sacraments. Its lapidary parallelism is marvellous. Making a parallel and even a poetic synonymity between the word *redemptio* and the word *adoptio,* it suggests that the action of redemption, or God's action in redeeming human beings, is at the same time the act of adopting them in love as children. From this there flow the fruits of redemption as listed in the Letter to the Galatians, true freedom and an eternal inheritance (Gal 4:1–7).

A final example is taken here from the old Roman collection, the Verona. The prayer appears to have been composed by Pope Vigilius at the time of the siege of Rome in 537–538 A.D. by the Arian Ostrogoths under Witiges.[31] In English translation, it reads:

> All powerful and merciful God,
> from whose gift it comes that you are served by your faithful
>   in a fitting and praiseworthy manner,

---

30. Moore, *Vatican II*, 223.
31. Ibid., 401.

bestow upon us, we ask you, that we may run to your
promises without offense.

In face of this affliction, it invites the people to turn in confidence
to God's power and mercy. It embodies the conviction that even
in troubled times worship continues, a worship that is worthy and
true, directed to the God known to Christians but called into question by the Arians. There is a nice inclusion in this prayer of the
way in which Christian devotion used sacrificial vocabulary in that
it asks that God be worshipped *laudabiliter,* or with due praise. This
evokes quite readily the common parlance of a worship that is at
its very core a sacrifice of praise, offered by children, not a rite of
retribution and the offering of holocausts.

In characterizing the tenor and qualities of all these prayers,
Moore notes that they reflect faith in a single economy of creation and
redemption and of the ultimate and expected completion of God's
work.[32] While, on the one hand, Roman religion is transformed into
a religion of love, which has its origin in God's benevolence and
dispensation of divine exchange, and while the prayers change the
notion and reality of ritual sacrifice, they also embrace a metaphorical construct of order and providence. Apart from the antiquity
of their style, the stress on orderly providence is hard to assimilate
into the memories which the Church today must embrace as it
remembers Christ and prays in his name; there is too much that
does not fit well into a conceived order of provident disposition.

The sense of order which runs through these Roman texts is
what provided the foundation for the ordered and hierarchical vision of Church, ministry, and liturgy which developed over time.
This priestly notion and practice of sacrifice could appeal to this
Roman foundation. In fact, of course, it is an interpretation and
development of the tradition that took place within social and ecclesiastical conditions that highly favored order. Today some people
look back on the age of Roman liturgy within the medieval Church
and society as a model for the reordering of our own times. It is
said that it was a time when all could be seen in the clear order
of creation and providence and each and all knew where they belonged in the cosmos and in the Church. That is true up to a point.
The vision helps us to understand the development of the liturgy

---

32. Ibid., 634.

under Carolingian and then under papal dominance. This, however, should not be too narrowly equated with the Roman liturgy
as it originated in the Church of Rome, and it does not provide a
good model for prayer and governance at the cusp of the millennium, however appealing it may be as we live through a disturbed
period of global communication.

The tradition of Roman prayer can then be summarized in several
points: (*a*) it uses forms worthy of public service, doing so according to an idiom known and respected by those who participate in it;
(*b*) it is artfully biblical and even through these forms depicts a worship fitting to those who venerate a God of love as his children and
in fitting words of praise and supplication rather than through sacrificial rites of pagan homage; (*c*) it responds to particular situations
of time and place and is the prayer of a Church that clearly belongs
in its own time and place; (*d*) it transforms the vocabulary of sacrifice and of the economy of exchange between God and humanity;
but (*e*) it also adopts a paradigm of ordered providence that relates
all God's actions to each other. What make these prayers hard to
appropriate today are their cultural idiosyncrasy and their perception of an untroubled order of divine action which overcomes all
human troubles. It is in the very recognition of these limitations that
the tradition may serve today as a model of liturgical composition
that is both culturally apt and profoundly biblical, and in organic
continuity with the most venerable prayer traditions of the history
of the Roman liturgy. In translating these prayers, a style has to be
found which makes them more suited to current rhetorical devices.
In praying them, introducing them (as presiders are invited to do),
and commenting upon them, it is not order that is best brought to
the fore but the more biblical images.[33] What is of more immediate concern in this work is the way in which the prayers suppose
acquaintance with the scriptures and the way in which they work
biblical images into their composition. This is in effect done so as
to relate a scripturally grounded faith to the realities and concerns
about life in its time which the congregation brings to its worship.

---

33. I do not intend to idealize these prayers as though no further cultural creativity
were possible. But this is a long-term task. The Roman prayers, along with some
new compositions of dubious value, are what our liturgical books provide. Hence
the concern here is to reach into this tradition and to place its usage within a new
context.

Table 5.1

Roman Collect[34]	Thomas Cranmer[35]	Alternative Service, 1980[36]
Almighty eternal God, who have consecrated [made holy] this day through the incarnation [taking on flesh] of your Word and through the giving birth of the virgin Mary, in this celebration of your justice [righteousness] give to your people that as they have been redeemed by your grace so may they be the children of your adoption.	Almighty God, who hast given us thy only-begotten Son to take our nature upon him, and as at this time to be born of a pure virgin; grant that we being regenerate and made thy children by adoption and grace, may daily be renewed by thy Holy Spirit.	All praise to you, almighty God and heavenly king, who sent your Son into the world to take our nature upon him and to be born of a pure virgin; grant that, as we are born again in him, so he may continually dwell in us and reign on earth as he reigns in heaven.

In addition to these qualities of the Latin text, the Anglican tradition shows us how the prayers can undergo some transposition when adapted for another language and another time. This is quite in keeping with the creativity inherent to the tradition, mostly because of the intensely biblical character of the prayers' words and imagery.

What we see is that as passed on over time, the collects can be given a transposition rather than a rigid repetition or translation. One good example may be found by comparing English versions of Christmas Day collects with the original Latin whence they derive. Table 5.1 offers a helpful comparative arrangement of the texts. The first column gives an old Roman collect from what is called the Gelasian Sacramentary. The second is Thomas Cranmer's elegant composition for *The Book of Common Prayer,* in which he transposes the Roman text. The third is the transposition of Cranmer's text into a modern prayer book, namely, *The Alternative Service Book* put together for the Church of England in 1980.

In each version of the prayer, the scriptural background is crystal clear. Whether it be the Johannine taking flesh of the Word or

---

34. I give this in a rather literal translation from the Latin.

35. This prayer is given as it stands in the 1979 *Book of Common Prayer* for the U.S. Episcopal Church. It is also found in the 1978 *Australian Book of Prayer,* with the one small change which replaces "regenerate" with "born again."

36. *The Alternative Service Book, 1980,* authorized for use in the Church of England (London and Cambridge: Clowes, SPCK, Cambridge University Press, 1980), 443.

the more Pauline sending of the Son to take on human nature, all three versions recall the mystery of the birth of Christ in scriptural terms. With this birth of the Word or Son of God, they parallel humanity's regeneration or rebirth as children of God. Perhaps it is to make this parallel clearer that Cranmer chose "Son" rather than "Word." It is not so easy to know why he prefers the more abstract "take our nature upon him" to "incarnation" or "taking on flesh." Cranmer and the Gelasian, but not the 1980 version, also make parallels between the working of God's grace in humanity and the adoption as children. To grace and adoption, the Anglican sources add the image of rebirth. To the initial redemptive act of grace, Cranmer adds the daily operation of the Holy Spirit in the Christian life.

The more recent adaptation of the prayer to the Anglican prayer book shows some concern with a contemporary rhetoric to replace that of Cranmer. The author is clearly interested in founding intercession to God in praise of God. There is also a reduction of the several metaphors which in the prayers of Rome and Cranmer express the work of grace to the single image of rebirth. On the other hand, for reference to the continual work of the Spirit it substitutes the images of Christ's indwelling and of his reign. This may well reflect a biblical and pastoral interest of the 1980s in the Gospel proclamation of the reign of God.

This transposition in some ways corresponds to the oral tradition of a Basotho poem mentioned in an earlier chapter. The tradition of prayer continues to use fundamental biblical images. Fidelity to the imagery and to the theology of incarnation and divine grace goes with a concern with a style appropriate first to another language and then to a later age. Each composition also reflects some particular interest. That of the Roman original is the liturgical celebration which marks the joy of the Feast of the Nativity. Cranmer's interest appears to be the theology of grace, since he omits any reference to the holiness of the day or to celebration. With its praiseful opening, the 1980 prayer regains some sense of joyful celebration but introduces an interest in the theology of Christ's reign.

Given then the breakdown of the sacrificial paradigm as a unifying force, it is asked whether within a different vision of Christ's place in human reality it is possible to draw otherwise on the ancient creativity here illustrated. That is the issue to be pursued in the following chapter.

Conclusion

In this chapter, the topic has been the way in which scripture carries over into liturgical prayer. While many different uses of scriptural imagery can be quoted, the principal point of interest was in the employment of a particular paradigm or root metaphor to hold a liturgical family together. With this in mind, it was observed that the metaphor of sacrifice no longer functions in the Roman Rite as adequately as it did in the past, and that for reasons having to do with culture and time. Since the heritage of the Roman liturgy is always with us, some observations were made about its inherent creativity in order to ask how we might still live out of this heritage in the midst of transition. All of this was put in relation to the anguish of our time in giving voice to memories of the past. Against this background, we can move on in the next chapter to look at root metaphors put forward as appropriate both to tradition and to life in the world in which we now live.

Chapter Six

A Liturgy Nourished from Gospel Roots

THE POLISH POET Czeslaw Milosz, in a poem entitled "Dante," expresses the agony of what it is to live in a time which lacks clarity of vision. Before the cosmic vision of the *Commedia*, what can one say? It seems as though today we inhabit a world different from that of our ancestors, unable to recognize or affirm their ideas, their vision, their modes of speech and music. The inborn desire for a "God-like domain," however, remains. The poet prays for the light to guide him in the search for such a home, in the search for the eternal pearl of great price.[1]

Even in liturgy and its appeal to scriptures, what our ancestors and their traditions have given us does not work all that effectively. What is lacking to current liturgical expression and development, in face of disillusionment with the modern world, is a key description of Christ's work of salvation to which the liturgy as a whole, and in all its parts, may be referred within a coherent and diversified vision. Within the appeal to the stories, images, and metaphors of a tradition discussed in the last chapter, there is the question of the *root metaphor*.

A metaphor is a description of reality that gives insight into its meaning and its prospects. It is sometimes taken to be simply an ornamental way of saying something that is known or of rhetorically dressing up reality so as to make it persuasive. In fact, it is a key usage of language that offers insight and gives a vision of truth, a way of relating to what is described. The title of John Milton's poem *Paradise Lost* is not meant to designate the factual story of what happened to Adam and Eve. It stands for the world in which

---

1. Czeslaw Milosz, "Dante," in *Provinces: Poems 1987–1991* (Hopewell, N.J.: Ecco Press, 1991), 65.

we live, giving a vision rooted in the Genesis story and using the key image of paradise. It tells us how the world is experienced when life is felt as the abyss between a desired and promised happiness and the sense of alienation which affects us, or what it is to have lost paradise.

Historical events themselves may generate metaphors that speak to a people's desire to continue to live out of an ideal of the past. In the United States, talk of the American Constitution no longer means purely the piece of paper and the process of framing a constitution for a newborn nation. It says that this people has enshrined a certain number of values to which at every moment it looks back in order to look forward. Americans may argue about what the articles of the Constitution mean or about the precise manner of applying them today. Yet persons who differ in their views on this will equally embrace the proclamation of this Constitution as the seedbed of life together as a nation. Within diversity, there is the commonality of an aspiration evoked by these two words.

If a metaphor is called a *root* metaphor, this is itself a metaphor, comparing language usage to the growth of a tree or a robust plant. The trunk, the bark, the branches, the leaves, and the fruit simply could not be unless they drew life from the roots. The term "American Constitution" does seem still to play such a role in American public life. Sometimes, however, what functioned as root metaphors lose their vitality. In Ireland, during the first fifty years of an independent state, the "Easter Rising" played this role. What happened in Easter Week 1916, the sacrifice of those who took up arms against a foreign domination, inspired the aspirations of the Irish people as a whole. Its usage recently, however, has suffered an eclipse. There is a disillusionment with the values and ideals of the leaders of the state during those years. There is the work of revisionist history that asks questions about the ideals and the actions of the men of Easter Week. For some, especially it seems poets, there is a move to look further back into the emergence of Celtic culture and into the meeting of this culture with that of new arrivals on the island. There is a general sense that economic advance itself does not produce a durable future. A new vision has to be bred, and it needs its rhetoric, its poetry, its fiction, its narratives, its metaphors.

The scriptures are full of such metaphors. The "kingdom of Israel" is not simply a designation of a period in the history of the Jewish people. It certainly arose as a powerful symbol under the

Davidic dynasty, but it retained its life even after the fall of the kingdom. It evokes and inspires an ideal grounded in the proclamation of the name of Yahweh. Under Christian auspices, the metaphor becomes simply the "reign of God" and suggests a more universal vision of a life between peoples grounded in the story of Israel and the preaching of Jesus. Jesus expanded on the commitment to the reign of God by telling parables, which are sometimes called extended metaphors because they project comparisons that offer insight into what it is to live by this commitment.

When we ask about metaphors that may give Christian faith and liturgy renewed life and power, as well as a sense of cohesion and coherence, we are not trying to invent something new, drawn for example from a technological realm. We are looking back to the scriptures and their acceptance into tradition to find what may be emerging as an image and a story that inspires vision in face of the question of what it means to be Christian at the cusp of the millennium. This is to ask about a fresh root metaphor.

We do not need one that imposes a homogeneous universal order, nor one that claims a clear theoretical vision of the universe and of redemption. It needs to be one that is open to temporal and cultural diversity and that gives Christians the faith and the inspiration to journey, to live with faith even in the midst of uncertainty. Some exploration of these possibilities is called for.

To engage in this pursuit, first we can look at the image of the Pasch or Passover that has been suggested in the course of the liturgical renewal that was affirmed and then fostered in the Catholic Church by the Second Vatican Council and its aftermath. Without discountenancing the service rendered by this mystagogical image, we can then turn to the image of divine *kenosis* that seems to carry weight in our time.

The Pasch of Christ and of the Christian

The Second Vatican Council in its document on the liturgy (*Sacrosanctum Concilium* [*SC*]) advanced the use of the metaphor of Pasch or Paschal Mystery. This first refers to the fact that it is through his Incarnation, Passion, death, resurrection, and glorious ascension (*SC* 5) that Christ redeemed humanity and that it is this memorial which is celebrated in the Church's liturgy. However, it is primarily a mystagogical term, meaning that through the liturgy the Church participates in the Pasch of Christ and that this offers a perception of how Christians are called to live when embodied in Christ (*SC* 6).

Nonetheless, when this metaphor is considered in its relation to its biblical roots and to early Christian tradition, it is not without ambiguity. In the text of Exodus 12, the image is introduced to signify the passing of the Lord, when the avenging angel passed over the houses marked by the blood of the Lamb. Elsewhere, this image of passage means the passing of the children of Israel to freedom through the Red Sea. When Paul calls on the Christians of Corinth to celebrate the new leaven, he says, "Christ our Pasch has been sacrificed," thus from the Exodus story recalling especially the immolation of the Lamb. Hence the term means either a passage from slavery to freedom, God's passing, or the blood sacrifice which is the sign of deliverance.

Looking to early Christian writers, there is with some, primarily Origen, an adherence to the understanding of Pasch as passage. Christ himself passed through death to life. In the sacramental mysteries, Christians are initiated into similar passage. Christian life itself is a constant passage, from darkness to the Father. Other writers, however, understand Pasch to refer to suffering, and what is then accentuated is that it was through suffering that Christ redeemed sinners and that biblically this is typified in all those who suffered in faith, such as the just Abel killed by Cain, Joseph sold by his brothers into slavery, or David beset by his enemies.[2]

In short, the image of Paschal Mystery in early Christian literature may contain three distinct metaphorical usages. One underscores the Paschal sacrifice with its sacrificial banquet. Another highlights the passage or transition effected by Christ himself and shared through the sacraments by those incorporated into him. A third speaks rather of the suffering through which Christ redeemed sinners.

It is not clear what life this metaphor retained in the official revision of liturgy after the council. The General Introduction to the Sacraments of Christian Initiation, preface to both adult and infant rites, does not use the term at all, though it does say that the

---

2. On this, see David N. Power, *Unsearchable Riches: The Symbolic Nature of the Liturgy* (New York: Pueblo, 1983), 154–56; idem, s.v. "Sacrament," in *The New Dictionary of Catholic Spirituality,* ed., Michael Downey (Collegeville, Minn.: Liturgical Press, 1993), 836–38.

baptized have died, been buried, and risen together with Christ.[3] The blessing of the baptismal water employs among other images the symbolism of the passage of the Israelite people through the Red Sea. In its reference to the crucifixion of Jesus Christ, it mentions the blood and water which flowed out from his pierced side, in which flow is seen the origin of the two sacraments of baptism and Eucharist. The rest of the liturgy uses such images as regeneration, light, and configuration to Christ through anointing. The Paschal imagery hardly plays a key role in this euchology.

The General Instruction of the 1975 Roman Missal passes over the image of Paschal Mystery and heavily accentuates the nature of the Mass as sacrifice, memorial of the one sacrifice of Christ on the cross, without any reference to the Pasch. When the eucharistic prayer adapted from the ancient text of the *Apostolic Tradition* refers to the death of Christ it is to uphold his victory over the power of death and of sin. The various prefaces for eucharistic prayers, found either for Sundays or for the feasts of saints, are medleys of images that are certainly not held together by a distinct Paschal reference.

One suspects that in liturgical catechesis, reference to the Pasch is used to strengthen the sense of the Church's sacramental participation in the mystery of Christ's Passion, death, and resurrection. However, there is an apparent lack of any strong and coherent Paschal imagery in liturgical texts to offer an awareness of what this means.

Lutheran Liturgy

In the revision of liturgical books undertaken by many Christian churches in recent decades, there is a remarkable convergence in the choice of scriptures and in many of the prayers used. This is partly because to some considerable extent churches have worked together and partly because all Western churches looked, to a greater or less degree, to the sources of the Roman Rite, prior to the later medieval and pre-Tridentine period.

It is worth noting some of the peculiarities of the Lutheran liturgy

---

3. For both of these texts, see International Commission on English in the Liturgy, ed., *Documents on the Liturgy 1963–1979: Conciliar, Papal, and Curial Texts* (Collegeville, Minn.: Liturgical Press, 1982), 465–67, 719–21.

to see how the Paschal imagery fits into it and how it relates to its own origins in Luther's reform of the Roman liturgy.

In the proper prefaces to the Great Thanksgiving Prayer in the U.S. *Lutheran Book of Worship*,[4] during the annual commemoration of the death and resurrection of Christ, the Paschal metaphor occurs chiefly in the image of the overcoming of death through the death and resurrection of Jesus Christ. Thus the preface for Passion Sunday reads, "on the tree of the cross [he] gave salvation to all, that, where death began, there life might be restored," while that for Easter says, "he is the true Passover Lamb who gave himself to take away our sin, who by his death has destroyed death, and by his rising has brought us to eternal life." Indeed, the preface for Sundays after Pentecost is quite similar: "[he] on this day overcame death and the grave, and by his glorious resurrection opened to us the way of everlasting life." The same book, in its notes on the meaning of the Vigil of Easter, has this to say:

> [This service] is full of contrast between darkness and light, death and life, chaos and order, slavery and freedom. The cross is vindicated as the Lord's throne, and the fulness of salvation finds expression—creation and redemption, old covenant and new covenant, baptism and Eucharist.[5]

The Lutheran service for the Easter Vigil has reinstated Exod 12:1–24 among the readings. It is there followed by this collect:

> Almighty and ever-living God, wonderful in all your works: Let your people understand that even more marvelous than the world's creation is your gift at the end of time: the sacrifice of our Passover Lamb, your Son, Jesus Christ, our Lord.

Earlier in the vigil, the collect following the reading of Exodus 14 relates the image of deliverance of the Israelite people to the waters of baptism, by-passing the image of passage. The final reading, before the canticle of Daniel 3, is from the song of Moses recounted in Deut 31:19–30. This is followed by a collect which incorporates some typical Lutheran themes:

---

4. *Lutheran Book of Worship: Minister's Desk Edition* (Minneapolis: Augsburg Publishing House, 1978), 211–17.

5. Ibid., 24.

O God, exaltation of the humble and strength of the righteous: You taught your people through Moses to sing your praise, that the law which [was] delivered to them might be helpful to us. Show your power among all nations that, in the forgiveness of sins, terror may turn to joy, and fear of retribution to salvation.[6]

Various references to the passage of the Jewish people are used in these texts, but as far as distinct Paschal imagery is concerned it is the Passover sacrifice of Christ which is to the fore, as this comes from Saint Paul.

What is here prayed may readily be related to Luther's own prayer for baptism, known as the Flood Prayer. There he invokes the idea of passage but underlines the faith necessary to salvation and the separation of the chosen from the unfaithful. The whole parade of images and metaphors can also be readily ordered and oriented to the meaning which Luther gave to the cross and to the Lord's Supper, as for example when he said about the paraphrase of the Lord's Supper within the communion service:

I admonish you in Christ that you discern the Testament of Christ in true faith and, above all, take to heart the words wherein Christ imparts to us his body and blood for the remission of our sins. That you remember and give thanks for his boundless love which he proved to us when he redeemed us from God's wrath, sin, death, and hell by his own blood. And that in this faith you externally receive the bread and wine, i.e. his body and his blood, as the pledge and guarantee of this.[7]

Here Martin Luther evokes the power of Christ's blood, but all is related back to the one affirmation of the righteousness of God and the forgiveness of sins offered to us through the cross of Christ. This is, however, the gift of God's love. In Christ he found "the love, the goodness, the sweetness of God, . . . the wisdom, the power and the

---

6. Ibid., 151.
7. Luther's service for the Lord's Supper, and this text in particular, can be readily found in R. C. D. Jasper and G. J. Cuming, eds., *Prayers of the Eucharist: Early and Reformed*, 3d ed. (Collegeville, Minn.: Liturgical Press, 1987), 197.

majesty of the sweet God placed at your disposition."[8] Christ is "the one who loves those who are in anguish, in sin and in death."[9]

It is in virtue of Christ's resurrection that we have a firm foundation for faith in his lordship and for his presence in the Lord's Supper. However, it is still through the revelation of his suffering that we perceive God's righteousness and our justification. He had already said in the theses for the Heidelberg disputation, "the one who beholds what is invisible of God, through the perception of what is made, is not rightly called a theologian (thesis 19). But rather the one who perceives what is visible of God's 'backside' (Exodus 33:23), by beholding the suffering and the Cross (thesis 20)."

In his works, to express how God's righteousness and forgiveness are made known to faith, Luther quotes 2 Cor 5:21: Christ crucified "is made sin for us, that we might be made the righteousness of God through him." It is in accordance with this that Christians exercise their priesthood, in life and in worship:

> Here we see that every Christian is a true priest: for first he offereth and killeth his own reason, and the wisdom of his flesh; then he giveth glory unto God that he is righteous, true, patient, pitiful and merciful. And this is the daily sacrifice of the New Testament which must be offered evening and morning.[10]

From all this we can see the appropriate place which the Good Friday liturgy, even in its more traditional and Roman forms, has in the Lutheran service. The two collects offered as alternatives for the opening of the day's liturgy, and which are taken from Roman sources, are centered in the images of Christ's being given over by betrayal to the hands of sinners and of the hanging of his body on the tree of the cross, both images obviously taken from the scriptures. Between the Lesson and the Passion Narrative, the service book provides for the singing of the hymn "O Sacred Head, Now Wounded."[11] This hymn as it stands is a Lutheran composition from the seventeenth century but derives from a poem written by Bernard of Clairvaux. The hymn extols Christ's suffering in all his body's members, but the last stanza reads:

---

8. Martin Luther, "Commentary on the Letter to the Galatians," in *Luther's Works* (Philadelphia: Fortress, 1955–), 40:26.

9. Ibid.

10. Ibid.

11. *Lutheran Book of Worship*, 138–39.

What language shall I borrow to thank thee, dearest friend,
for this thy dying sorrow, thy pity without end?
O make me thine forever; and should I fainting be,
Lord, let me never, never outlive my love to thee.

Some might claim that it is wrong to talk of *justification* as a metaphor, since this is what really happens. However, reality and metaphor do not cancel each other out. We need the power of metaphorical language to convey the reality, to express what it is. Martin Luther in his theology combined strong christological images with his doctrine of justification by faith, images that play a strong role in worship. The basic affirmation, or root metaphor, is that we are justified only by faith, only by the justice that is given to us in Christ. It was on account of this belief that Luther set about discrediting what he found to be a reliance on works and on the works of a cultic priesthood in late medieval thought and practice.[12] In speaking of the work of Christ, he resorts in some fashion to the theology of Saint Anselm, which postulates the need for a sacrifice that makes satisfaction for sins and so resorts to penal metaphors to explain the work of redemption. However, he also uses earlier Christian images, those found in early Paschal homilies and indeed in the Roman liturgy itself, which picture the cross of Christ as a duel between life and death, a duel in which life is victorious. This affirmation of victory and belief in the lordship of Christ does not take over in Luther, for in his theology he always emphasized that God is known to us in the suffering of the cross, in being hidden to us in this agony. It may well be that it is in the accent on faith in what is given to us in Christ and on the concealment of divine glory on the cross that Luther's theology and Lutheran worship make way for a greater liturgical accentuation of self-emptying, of a divine *kenosis* that is in fact an act that emanates purely and simply from God's great love.[13]

The image of Christ's self-emptying, or *kenosis*, has a clear place in Luther's writings. In many places, such as "The Bondage of the Will" and "The Freedom of a Christian,"[14] Martin Luther appeals

---

12. To us now his reading of the Roman canon seems to be a misreading of the original canon itself, but it is a reading in the cultic context of the times.

13. There is an illuminating presentation of Luther's theology of the cross by Gerhard O. Forde, "The Work of Christ," in *Christian Dogmatics,* ed. Carl E. Braaten and Robert W. Jenson (Philadelphia: Fortress, 1984), 2:5–99.

14. See the English translation of these two works in *Martin Luther's Basic*

to the words of the hymn in Philippians. Jesus emptied himself of glory and took on the form of a servant for the sake of sinners. Luther pursues this image to say that Christ became like sinners, or took on sin and all its consequences, in humble obedience to his Father and to save humankind from sin. This is the utmost outpouring of love. Luther also says that those who live by faith in Christ, who find the promise of forgiveness and justification in his cross, who learn to rely on this and on nothing else, will themselves act out of love for others. They too will empty themselves of all vain glory; they will learn to serve others and suffer for others. Works of this sort do not justify them, for only faith in Christ justifies, but they are the outcome of faith, the outcome of their union with Christ in faith.

Book of Common Worship

The introduction to the recently published book of worship for Presbyterian churches in the United States[15] is, like most recent revisions of liturgy, highly practical in the sense that it retrieves ancient practices as well as those of the Reformed tradition, and that its editors had an eye on ecumenical convergences. The theological direction of the services is, however, expressed in the introduction:

> An important characteristic of worship in the Reformed tradition is that it centers on God rather than ourselves and our feelings. Our attention is drawn to the majesty and glory of the triune God, who created all things and by whose power all things are sustained, who was revealed in Jesus Christ raised from the dead to rule over all things, and who is at work as the giver of life in and among us by the power of the Holy Spirit.[16]

In its service for the Great Vigil of Easter, the prayer book opens with an appeal to the image of Passover in these opening words of the presiding minister:

Theological Writings, ed. Timothy F. Lull (Minneapolis: Fortress, 1989), 173–223, 585–629.

15. *Book of Common Worship*, prepared by the Theology and Worship Ministry Unit for the Presbyterian Church (U.S.A.) and the Cumberland Presbyterian Church (Louisville: Westminster/John Knox Press, 1993).

16. Ibid., 8.

Sisters and brothers in Christ,
on this most holy night
when our Savior Jesus Christ passed from death to life,
we gather with the church throughout the world
in vigil and prayer.
This is the Passover of Jesus Christ:
Through light and the Word,
through water and the bread and wine,
we recall Christ's death and resurrection,
we share Christ's triumph over sin and death,
and with invincible hope
we await Christ's coming again.

The clear interpretation of the Pasch of Christ in these words is that of Passover, or passage from death to life, though his triumph over sin and death is also recalled. The version of the Easter proclamation at the lighting of the Paschal candle focuses on the proclamation of Christ as King, the one who has conquered darkness. The readings from the scriptures are the ones that have been long traditional in the West. Thus while Exodus 14 on the passage through the Red Sea is given, Exodus 12 on the Passover Lamb is not. As in the Roman Rite, this reading is included in a eucharistic celebration for Maundy Thursday. The interpretation given in the collect after Gen 22:1–18 interprets the action of Abraham as an act of obedience through which God's faithful love was made known, and this is then linked to the "grace of Christ's sacrifice" in which is given the promise of a new covenant. The hymn to Christ of Philippians 2 is used on Passion or Palm Sunday, in conjunction with the reading of the Passion from one of the Synoptic Gospels and with the song of the suffering servant in Isa 50:4–9a.

The many texts for the Great Thanksgiving Prayer of the Eucharist offered in this book of worship are quite varied and settle on no prevailing image or images. It is of interest to note, however, that the first in the book, Prayer A, is grounded in the Eastern images of the Father sending the Son out of love for sinful humanity and of the Son's victory over death in his rising from the grave.

In writing of justification in the *Institutes of the Christian Religion,* John Calvin presented the doctrine of justification by faith

alone and of the imputation of Christ's righteousness to sinners.[17]
He has occasion there to refer to the Pauline texts on the death of
Christ in which Paul writes of Christ's suffering and of his taking
on sin for us. He also makes mention of the transfusion of Christ's
power to the justified, and it is this on which he elaborates in the
part of the *Institutes* on the Lord's Supper, where he celebrates the
"wondrous exchange" brought about:

> This is the wondrous exchange made by his boundless good-
> ness. Having become with us the Son of Man, he has made
> us with himself sons of God. By his own descent to the earth
> he has prepared our ascent to heaven. Having received our
> mortality, he has bestowed on us immortality. Having under-
> taken our weakness, he has made us strong in his strength.
> Having submitted to our poverty, he has transferred to us his
> riches. Having taken upon himself the burden of unrighteous-
> ness with which we were oppressed, he has clothed us with
> his righteousness.[18]

The closest that the Eucharist of the *Book of Common Worship*
comes to this vision of wondrous exchange is Great Thanksgiving G,
which is its transposition of the prayer from the *Apostolic Tradition*.
Thus like all other prayer book revisions, the Presbyterian tradition
helpfully recalls a long Christian tradition and helps us to celebrate
the full mystery of Christ's Pasch in his Incarnation, death, resurrection, and ascension. Like others also, however, there is no clear
or dominant slant on this mystery that serves to give focus or vision
to the whole.

This cursory glance at revised books of worship in three Church
traditions helps to put forward the issue of root metaphor which
this chapter addresses. It is not the intention that any of the rich
tradition of the ages should be eliminated, nor that only one of the
scripture's metaphors should take over from others. The point made
is rather that though different Christian churches and different ages

---

17. John Calvin, *Institutes of the Christian Religion*, trans. Henry Beveridge
(Grand Rapids, Mich.: Wm. B. Eerdmans Publishing Company, 1989), bk. 3,
chap. 12. Whenever Calvin refers to Philippians 2, it is to speak of the two natures
in Christ.

18. Ibid., bk. 4, chap. 17, 2. The eucharistic prayer in the *Book of Common
Worship* that is closest to this vision of worship is its rendering of the prayer of the
Apostolic Tradition. See *Book of Common Worship*, Great Thanksgiving G, 150–51.

had this copious plenty in hand, there is always some need to give it focus through a particular image or metaphor that interprets the parts and the whole. In the history of the Roman Rite, this was the image of sacrifice. In the Byzantine, it was the image of the loving sending of the Son. For Martin Luther, it is the testament of the forgiveness of sins offered to the faith of those who come to him as their only righteousness. For Calvin, when it comes to worship it is the mystery of wondrous exchange that is celebrated.

The metaphor of Pasch is now often put forward as key to worship. Its power is not here denied, but the references to the worship books of several Christian traditions at this millennium cusp show how indeterminate it is. What is proposed then is the power that the image of Christ's *kenosis* may have as an interpretative or root metaphor for people who find memory and prayer difficult because of memories.

The Root Metaphor of *Kenosis*

This may well serve as a powerful metaphor whereby to gather together and to penetrate use of other images and interpretations in relating the hearing of scriptural texts to liturgical action and to the Christian life. A new and appropriate attention to it has been suggested by biblical scholars, by postmodern writers, and even by the Roman magisterium. Theological reflection on this has, as seen, been augured by Pope John Paul II. It may well be taken up also by the practice and speech of worship in the Church.

We can first look at the more significant biblical texts where the image is found or to which it is related. Then, it can be asked what it offers to make prayer possible in a time of horror when memory is difficult. Finally, to test its efficacy, rather tentatively as is fitting, we may ask how reference to it would help a congregation to listen to, interpret, and respond to the scriptural readings of the Paschal Vigil.

Kenosis

The image and metaphor of *kenosis*, or self-emptying, derives from Phil 2:5–11.[19] Its meaning, however, and the extent of its influ-

---

19. For an overview of interpretations, see Frank Matera, *New Testament Christology* (Louisville: Westminster/John Knox Press, 1999), 120–31. See also Lucien Richard, *Christ: The Self-Emptying of God* (New York and Mahwah, N.J.: Paulist Press, 1997), 56–72.

ence are not wholly determined by this passage. As a good root metaphor, it can gather in many other biblical texts and scatter its influence through many an utterance.

The passage in Philippians comes from the writer's quotation, and possible mutation, of a popular hymn to Christ. It is used by Paul as motivation for a moral exhortation to humility. Its power, however, overflows that application, and it is now in fact used as a root metaphor in some systematic Christologies.[20]

The text itself relates Christ's appearance in the flesh, his death on the cross, and his role in the Church as Lord, or Kyrios. The images used to illuminate these events are self-emptying, humiliation through obedience, and exaltation.

The self-emptying is identical with the manner in which Christ appeared in the flesh. He could have wished to reflect majesty, power, and dominion in his earthly existence. Instead he identified himself with that which is most lowly, vulnerable, and mortal in human life. Indeed, he appears as a slave, the most lowly of servants, putting himself into the service of his sisters and brothers. Some commentators see this as a way of contrasting Christ with Adam, following out a favored Pauline motif. Adam, according to the Genesis story and its interpretation, sought to make the most of his dominion over the earth, whereas Christ, second Adam, offers himself as a slave. Others see reference to Christ's preexistence and divinity. The Son of God, divine in his preexistence, now takes on human flesh and in so doing goes to the extreme of appearing in servitude to others. In either interpretation, it is the act of self-emptying which is highlighted, a readiness to cast aside all pretense to show or to domination over others. It is highlighted as a generous gift, something that comes forth from a divine fullness, and in its very humility carries into the world the overflow of such fullness.

The image of being slave or servant is a natural lead into a representation of the death on the cross as an act of humility, indeed as Christ's supreme humiliation. It is not simply that he chose to be mortal, to suffer the mortality of all human creatures. In subjecting himself willfully to death on the cross, Jesus was enslaved to hostile powers and exposed to indignity, in consequence of his opposition to powers that dominate either through religious influence or through temporal dominion. This very act is a revelation

---

20. See Richard, *Christ: The Self-Emptying of God.*

of the divine, showing itself in the flesh of Christ. It manifests an ungrasping, bounteous, generous, overflowing love of which only the divine is of itself capable, while it also contrasts the exercise of the divine power of love with the claims of earthly powers.

This leads to the image of exaltation. The hymn locates this in Christ's endowment with the name of Kyrios, or Lord. Through his self-emptying life in the flesh and through the humiliation of the cross, Jesus has been given access to the mediation of God's power to the Church and to the world. It is in virtue of his self-emptying and obedience, and in virtue of its remembrance and proclamation, that Christ is now present in the Church as Lord.

The moral exhortation to humility among the members of the Church flows from this. For Christ's followers, *kenosis* means to live together as servants, each at the service of the other. It means setting aside claims and aspirations to dominate and lord it over others. It is to turn away from empty show of force and constraint.

1 Corinthians 2:7

The text to which Pope John Paul allies the image of *kenosis* is 1 Cor 2:1–13, with special reference to 2:2 and 2:7. The word which Paul speaks "about Jesus Christ who has been nailed to a cross" is "God's hidden and mysterious wisdom." This is the one wisdom by which Paul wishes the disciples to live. It is put in contrast with the wisdom of the exact observance of the Law and with the wisdom of philosophy (1 Cor 1:23–24). These are ways in which it is possible to seek happiness and salvation. The one true way, however, shown by God is the wisdom of the cross.

Sacrifice

The metaphor of *kenosis* also does justice to, and interprets, the designation of Christ's death as a sacrifice in the New Testament and thus frees it from later, superimposed, cultic, and hierarchical interpretations. In the letters of Paul there are some quite specific texts wherein the author explains what Christ did for us through his death by using the cultic and sacrificial vocabulary of the Old Testament code of sacrifices. In 1 Cor 5:7 there is the simple and straightforward affirmation, "Christ, our paschal lamb, has been sacrificed." Of more significance are the texts in which Paul speaks of Christ's death as a "sin-offering": Rom 3:24; 8:3; 2 Cor 5:21.

The context into which to put these texts is provided by Paul's explanation of the representative character of Jesus and of his death. It is as the second Adam, as the one for all, that he submits to death at the Father's will. This is an initiative that comes from God in his gracious mercy. It is the act whereby Jesus himself took on sin. It is the act whereby God, in his Son made flesh, makes sinners righteous. The levitical code of sacrifice and worship is surpassed and outmoded by the death of Christ. It is not by cultic offerings that humankind is to be justified but through the death of Christ in the flesh. The atonement sought through sacrifices, and in a special way through the liturgy of Yom Kippur, has been given to us in Christ and through his death in the flesh. God has sent his own Son in the flesh, God has made him sin so that in him we might become the righteousness of God. Sending his Son in the likeness of sinful flesh, God has done what the Law in its weakness could not do.

In brief, the death of Christ may be called a sacrifice which God has provided in the sense that it is through it that sin is laid low and that God's justice or righteousness is given to a sinful humanity. Christ, though being without sin, has taken on the burden of sin in the flesh and has been subjected to death. The *kenosis* of God and of Christ is inherent to this meaning of sacrifice. Without such self-emptying, such divine gift, this atonement, this sacrifice, would have been impossible.

It is in the Letter to the Hebrews that cultic vocabulary comes to the fore in the proclamation of the death of Christ. What is affirmed in this letter is that the Temple liturgy is no longer operable. Jesus is the mediator of the new covenant, its high priest, its sacrificial offering. What is most fundamental in the letter is the proclamation of Jesus as the Son of God. As God's Son, he took on flesh and made himself one with the sufferings of humanity. It is as Son that he is mediator, priest, and offering. What the Temple cult sought to do, that is, to make atonement and to have access to God, Jesus has done in the flesh. By his death he has penetrated the veil of the flesh to the right hand of God, where he sojourns as priest for ever. In highlighting the sonship of Jesus, the author also highlights his suffering and what he learned in the flesh. It is this which makes sense of calling his death a sacrifice and which allows him to penetrate the heavens as offering, priest, and mediator.

In brief, what makes fundamental sense in these texts about the taking on of flesh and about the death of Jesus is the metaphor of self-emptying, of willing humiliation in the service of humankind. But Jesus does not simply act as a representative of humankind in face of God. He has been made such by God. The sacrifice of atonement, the access to God, the righteousness of the redeemed, is a gift from God. One with the image of *kenosis* is the image of giving, of gift, of the divine self-gift, the overflow of love that reveals itself in the folly of a service that appears alien to the human dispositions that prevail.

Indeed, this language has always belonged in the celebration of the Pasch of Christ's death and resurrection. The hymn of the Letter to the Philippians is found in the liturgy of Palm Sunday, with a response from Psalm 91. During the Holy Week Triduum, the Roman Office for centuries has sung the antiphon which paraphrases the hymn, *Christus factus est pro nobis,* Christ has become obedient for us, even unto death, even to the death of the cross, and on this account God has exalted him and given him a name above every name.

To grasp the import of this metaphor, Christ has to be remembered in his drinking of death even to its dregs. On the cross, he was one with the most desolate of victims, he himself the victim of betrayal and of the failure of love in his followers. He was the weakest of things, a worm, and hardly human. This is the sign of his complete oneness with humanity. In this sign, he continues to be present among those whose stories we find it so hard to reckon. It is an act which is indeed a self-emptying of the divine self and the divine image. God can no longer be known by the names and images which glorify his might, his power, his majesty. These images will continue to be used but subordinately to the image of a love-inspired *kenosis*. The only place to recognize the transmutation of divine powers is on the cross and among the ignoble of the earth. Indeed in Mark 9:30–37 it is narrated that Jesus' response to the quarrel over greatness among his disciples was to place a child in their midst and to invite them to welcome him in this child. This is to take as the very presence of Christ the presence of the weakest of the earth. Elsewhere (Mark 10:16), he tells them that they themselves must become as little children, that is, to let themselves be seen as weak in order to show forth the power of Christ's death.

This is the "grace of love"; this is what proclaims that human suffering is not "beyond love," however awkward and self-denying the speech in which it is voiced. When we in faith receive the Gospel of God's self-emptying in Christ, as the act of his love by which he gives us his Son, we cannot fail to acknowledge that all is gift. In a period when we witness not only the failure of human effort, power, and institutions, but their cruelty, witting or unwitting, we know that we must needs resort to God's love, God's justice, God's grace, as that on which, within and beyond human act and weakness, we have to rely. The Church's institutions and ministries themselves are but fragile messengers of God. They may proclaim the cross and ritually create the boundaries of our existence, but it is always beyond them that the eyes of faith look. Even when they fail, faith can still look to Christ and to his gift. It can acknowledge its continuing presence in the weak and in the forms of weakness.

Kenosis *and Liturgy: Prayer in a Time of Horror*

What may then be said of the appeal to this metaphor when memory is threatened by the unspeakable? To see the depths of its appeal to faith, I will suppose congregations that are aware of how much the AIDS pandemic marks our time. Together with the memory of the Holocaust, this affects our global age, for now and for the future, even more bitterly and deeply than the 1845 Irish famine marked the present and the future of Irish life and society in its time. Since it is global, the dimensions of the calamity are of course much greater. It shows that all our scientific exploration, including the mapping of the human genome, does not offer humans control of life and death. It presents the failure of globalization when this gets beyond the benefits reaped in the commercial and military worlds. It calls for a community of peoples that bonds in face of near despair, sensitive to the affliction visited on nations, on the poor, on women and children. To people of religious faith, it asks the question, Where is God?

Images of divine order and providence do not respond well to the situation. The image of passage through death to life, as it is now frequently interpreted in current liturgical catechesis, is inadequate. Indeed, it risks being mocking. Christ's offering of his life in sacrifice for the redemption of the world leaves wide open the question of how his redemption succors the suffering, who are without sin and who dwell still in the midst of death.

We have already seen in some Irish poets the perception that any nation's particular suffering must lead it to take on suffering on a larger scale, in memory and in looking forward. We have also seen suggested in them how humanity must bond with earth, must take on its suffering and its hopes. We have seen too the search for a speech that, even as it speaks, recognizes that what it speaks of is beyond speech. In Eavan Boland, we have found the faith that what is beyond speech is not "beyond love."

To draw inspiration from these orientations for the sacramental and liturgical expression and ritual of our faith in Christ, we can do a couple of things. We can prospect some strategies for speech. We can then ask how the language of *kenosis* may provide a language that gathers and scatters. This can later be tested by reference to the Paschal Vigil.

The Perils of Language

In being mindful of AIDS, those who suffer from it, those who have died of it and of human neglect, or of the disasters that we often dare not remember, we need to avoid certain modes of speech that come to the fore all too readily. First, we must avoid any hint of millennarism, about whose inadequacy enough has been said in writing of the Irish famine. Second, while we may with the Book of Revelation see these victims "under the altar" of our worship, we should avoid speaking of them as martyrs. This only misrepresents the nature and manner of their suffering and disallows any protest that we might address to God. Third, a purification of memories is required. Human failure and the prevalence of the forces of evil, in nature and in human societies, have to be acknowledged, and the churches cannot dodge the judgment that may also fall on them. Memory is false when it attributes causes to "others" or to some order of things. It has to admit sorrow, distress, and contrition within the recollection of the past. Fourth, the suffering and the dead are not to be left nameless, to be seen simply as categories of persons. This happens all too often in the stories of war, plague, famine, and other catastrophes that punctuate the history of the human race. Fifth, faith has to admit its lack of knowledge, and our memories and our prayer must needs hold back from "giving meaning" to these horrors, by placing them within an order of things to which we can give credit. This is the surest and most tempting way of not letting them remain "beyond speech."

The Strategies of Journey without Maps

"Strategies" suggests too much that is planned with an end in view. Hence, the word is here in part blocked out by saying that through liturgy today we are invited to embark on a journey with Christ to a Jerusalem that is not on the map. We might simply say that we are looking for paths to follow into the brush, paths on which we seek Christ present in his weakness and in his weak members.

One path to follow is that of keeping memory of all those for whom we wish God's loving salvation, as we find this expressed for us in the image of his gift and his presence among us in the self-emptying of Christ. Clearly, it is not for us to impose the Christian faith on those who have suffered and died in another tradition. However, for us as Christian communities the memorial of Christ is a memorial of God's loving embrace of all humanity and of his gift of life to all peoples. In this belief, our remembrance of Christ is a remembrance of a universal divine love to which in him we can give voice.

The insertion of the memories of victims of human folly, injustice, and hatred into the liturgy has its precedent in tradition. It was common in an earlier age to read the Acts of Martyrs, especially of the local church, within the liturgy of the Eucharist. This was a complement to the reading of the scriptures, especially the Gospel. For communities of remembrance, their strength in suffering and their witness were testimony to the living presence of the risen Jesus Christ in his Church, in a way that still kept his cross and suffering to the fore. Even in his risen glory and power, it is in the sick and the poor, for whom the collection was made, and in those who faced death in faith and trust, that he is to be found a living presence.

Churches today have introduced a new practice of witness and remembrance which provides a sort of model. Particularly during Paschaltide, neophytes and their sponsors give witness at the liturgy to the work of Christ's grace and Spirit. On other occasions also, perhaps when appeal is being made to members of the community to take up some ministry, those who minister and those to whom they minister may be asked to speak of this as an experience of grace and of God's gifts. At community liturgies for the anointing of the sick, both the sick and those who care for them can speak of how Christ is experienced in sickness. While certainly eulogies at funerals and wakes can get out of hand, there is some place to be mindful at such time of the journey through life of the deceased. In this case, another must speak in the person's name, embracing the dead one still as a member of the community of hope.

There are, however, few attempts, it seems, to remember the

forgotten dead, the victims who died without care and often in suffering and neglect, and of whom no fitting memory has been kept. That this be done is vital to living the Christian faith in the world of today. How it is to be done is not all that clear, but the foregoing shows that remembrance and testimony at Mass and at other liturgies have their precedents.

A vague and generic memory is inadequate. The remembered are not to be left nameless. At the Vietnam Memorial Wall in Washington, D.C., a monument to that most senseless of wars, there is a long list of names that respects this truth. In the Holocaust Memorial Museum in the same city, each visitor is provided with a passport on which there is a name of one of the victims. They are asked in this way to journey with this person through the memory of what happened, seeing it in ways that affected individual persons and families and neighborhoods and not just masses of unnamed people, or categories such as Jews, Gypsies, or handicapped. With the naming, there have to go testimonies. As far as possible, the dead who could not speak in their time have to be allowed voice. We listen to stories, to poems written in the midst of death. Sometimes the testimony—like that composed by Nelly Sachs, Paul Celan, and Primo Levi about the Holocaust—was written after the calendar time of history but by people who still within themselves continued to live out the tragedy. Sometimes, the living, the survivors, must dare take on the voice of the victims as Jeremiah did in his book of lamentations over Jerusalem or as psalmists did as though the writer was David in the midst of defeat and affliction.

Christians need to listen to the testimonies of Jewish victims in their liturgies. This is necessary to that purification of memories called for by Jubilee 2000. There are now testimonies in abundance and even interfaith prayer services where Jews and Christians together keep memory. All of this is available to Christians who listen to the Gospels. Some of them might be a very necessary complement to the reading of the Gospel of John during the Great Ninety Days from Lent to Pentecost. As we know, the Church is still only learning how to overcome its prejudices and to listen to Jewish voices.[21]

---

21. See the document of the U.S. Catholic Conference of Bishops, *God's Mercy Endures Forever: Guidelines on the Presentation of the Jews and Judaism in Catholic Preaching* (Washington, D.C.: USCC, 1988). For examples of prayer texts, see Elie Wiesel and Albert H. Friedlander, *The Six Days of Destruction: Meditations toward Hope* (New York and Mahwah, N.J.: Paulist Press, 1988); Irving Green-

It has to divest itself of many of its claims to power in order to make room for these voices.

Comparably, though of course in a different way, the liturgy must hearken to and incorporate the voices of witnesses to the AIDS pandemic. Little has yet been collected of these testimonies, so there is a task ahead for Christian communities. At the writing of these lines in July 2000, an international conference on AIDS was being held in Durban, South Africa. Most of the discussion was technical, medical, and statistical, as needs must be. However, on the margins some testimonies were being gathered. These are testimonies to be heard at liturgy, joined to the liturgy of the Word, much as we now listen in Eastertide to the witness given by neophytes and their sponsors or as of old people listened to the Acts of the Martyrs. In all of this we strain to hear the genius of an unnamed hope. This is what Eavan Boland does when seeing the stricken mothers with their dying and dead children, she sees in the vision "the grace of love."

One of those who spoke to the gathering at the AIDS conference was an eleven-year-old Zulu boy, Nkosi, who has since died. As he said, "I am an infected child. I have AIDS." He spoke of what it means to keep on living, as an orphan but fortunate enough to have an adoptive mother, unlike millions of others. While he asked for medical care for all, his main plea was that those infected like him be treated as human persons, given their dignity and respect. "Do not be afraid of us," he said, knowing that the ill were often shunned not out of malice but out of fear. He invited people to talk to the infected, to visit them, to show them care and love, even if they could bring them no cure. It is not necessary to have medicine in hand in order to talk to the sick. They can be approached as human persons. What a complement such testimony would be to the hearing of the scene of the last judgment or to any of the stories of how Jesus healed the ill of his time, or approached the lepers kept at a distance by those who feared their approach, or took sin upon himself.

Another story recounted was that of a woman, whose name was not given, who was told that in taking a certain medication, she needed to drink ten glasses of water per day. "In my village," she

---

berg and David Roskies, *A Holocaust Commemoration for Days of Remembrance* (Washington, D.C., 1981).

said, "we do not have that much clean drinking water." An Anglican priest from Uganda, Gideon Byamugisha, spoke of being HIV-positive, alluding to himself as "one of the 34 million HIV carriers." He told of the work that he and others were doing through their Christian ministry, but in collaboration with others, to bring the country to an awareness of this pandemic and to assist sufferers, most of whom are impoverished. Sadly he commented that some of the greatest prejudice which he encountered was among priests and ministers of the Christian churches. Other testimonies on the margins of the conference told of orphans and the care which some people, in their own small way, try to give to those left without mother or father because of their deaths due to AIDS.

And where is Christ? The Gospel has given us a response to this in the scene of the last judgment. He is there in the victims, one with them, we might say even one of them. Today when the language of evangelization is also the language of inculturation, the metaphors of incarnation and Trinitarian communion are used to give name to what is taking place.[22] It is said that Christ, the Word and Son of God, takes flesh anew among different peoples as he took flesh of the Jewish race. Completing this with the image of Trinity, it is said that the Incarnation itself in all its forms is a work of love, of a love that emanates from within the communion of Father, Son, and Spirit. These images may be fittingly applied to the presence of Christ among the suffering and the dead, whose memories are not yet released from their affliction. He takes body among them, the wounds of his flesh that he showed to his disciples being their wounds.

The Paschal Vigil Revisited

To test the power of the metaphor, I will now ask how it may serve a congregation as interpretative medium in listening to the texts of the Paschal Vigil and in entering into the prayer of sacramental commemoration.

Hearing the Scriptures

Does it make any difference in listening to Exodus 12, Exodus 14, Genesis 22, and Genesis 1 to let the story of Christ and of God's

---

22. *African Synod: Documents, Reflections, Perspectives*, comp. and ed. Africa Faith and Justice Network under the direction of Maura Browne, SND (Maryknoll, N.Y.: Orbis Books, 1996), 96, proposition 28.

presence be translated for us through the image of a self-emptying that finds a dwelling place among the sorrowing?

In listening to the Gospel of Easter Night, we might well give a preference to the story as recounted in Mark's Gospel. The women go to the tomb to anoint the body of the dead Christ. They see the tomb empty and are met by the angel who tells them that he is no longer among the dead. The women return home but dare not tell the story to anyone, not even to Jesus' disciples who ate and drank with him and saw him die, "from afar." That in this death and burial there might be the promise of resurrection, of an end to death itself, is too much to hear and impossible to say. As we see the Christ continue to be buried in his members, in those whom he loved even unto death, we may well find it hard to put words on faith in the resurrection, knowing that it is out of the proclamation of the death that the words of hope have to emerge.

As the congregation listens to the Genesis story of creation, of the emergence of cosmos from chaos, it may well find itself anew in the time of chaos, looking for the divine hand in bringing about a new creation for an afflicted and chaotic world. The promise is there and is received, but the order is for now beyond perception.

Of Genesis 22, the story of the binding of Isaac, it has already been said how it confronts us with the cruelty meted on the young in our age, with the loss of children that puts a stamp on what the world endures, with despair over progeny. The identification of Christ with Isaac takes a different turn to the wonted typology. The faith of Abraham and of those who find in him their "father in faith" is tried anew, in ways that it is impossible to escape.

Exodus 12 to 14 carry a story of deliverance from captivity and death, a story that is full of promise but which leaves the generation that passes from Egypt a generation that never sees the promises. The religious dimension of its presentation in the Pentateuch needs to be fully appreciated. This has to do with God's choice of Israel and the worship of the one true God by one people in the midst of polytheistic peoples. Their subjugation is related to this, and their deliverance is related to this. The image of a bellicose and slaughtering God is not the purpose of the text. Theirs is, however, a liberation that is won at the price of many deaths, of the destruction of the Egyptians, of those who could not be counted as sisters and brothers, in return of course for their own disavowal of these

Israelite refugees and their opposition to their belief in Yahweh, the one God of all.

The story conjures up for a congregation mindful of death's ways the stories of conflict and enmity in the midst of which they are compelled to search for the hand of God, in a world that often looks away from God. In the story of Christ, God's Son, the congregation is told that he is with all and any who are victims of the quest for power and dominance. Even the Egyptian foot soldiers and charioteers were but pawns in the strategies of Pharaoh. Thinking of the conflicts of our time, what does this say of the presence of the One who emptied himself unto death and who now is known among the dying and the dead, whoever they may be? What is it to profess faith in the love of the one true God who embraces all, in a world that looks for its future in other, more human-centered persuasions and strategies? To be baptized into Christ is to be baptized into this faith, and into a communion of love for which we are still searching.

Praying the Prayers

What may then be said of the proclamation of prayer texts at the vigil? Here are some orientations for the daring of such an act.

Blessing of the Paschal Candle

There are two things to be borne in mind for the commencement of the vigil with this rite. First, there is the sense of keeping vigil, second the origins of the prayer of blessing.

The blessing is indeed prayed to introduce a vigil that is scheduled for the hours of the night. In many places today this is not done, for practical reasons and to avoid keeping people out in the dangerous night hours. As far as possible, and with all necessary precautions, communities capture the sense of their vigil more powerfully by keeping watch through the night hours. Traditionally, night vigils were symbolic of eschatological expectation, especially the one which prepared for the Easter dawn and celebrated the resurrection of Christ. The Paschal Vigil brought to term the prayer by the tomb of Christ when all were mindful of his descent into the abode of the dead, of his embrace of the full rigors of death in solidarity with mortal humanity. Watching through the night, the Church took comfort and hope in the power of Christ to overcome darkness with his light, and to overcome death by his combat and resurrection. The full mystery of this mortal combat was expressed in the readings, psalms, and hymns, the memorial always affected by the hope of resurrection. The lighting of the lamps or candles that introduced the vigil recalled the mystery, praising the light that continues to shine in the time of darkness and anticipating the splendor of a luminous dawn.

The history of Christian night vigils tells us that in the time of Ambrose and Augustine, they were sometimes called when the Church was confronted by calamity and danger.[23] This could be heresy or it could be armies threatening to invade the city. Christians identified readily in the hour of peril with the symbolism of darkness and looked more eagerly to Christ for light as they sought protection and sought a clear path to follow. While this is not the particular sense of the Paschal Vigil, it does suggest how this vigil, in the larger tradition of vigils, may well express the anxiety of Christians in times and eras, such as ours, which are overshadowed by dark images and memories.

In line with this sense of keeping vigil, it can also be borne in mind that the tradition behind the blessing of the candle is the tradition of providing light with lamps and candles at evening prayer, and of blessing God at that moment with an appropriate prayer. This light, either an oil lamp or a wax candle made with wicks from straw, served the practical purpose of giving the light needed for evening prayer or, on occasion, for a vigil service leading into the first morning light. While the evening hymn with the onset of darkness looked to Christ as light, it was paired with morning hymns which when darkness receded celebrated Christ as the rising sun. The imagery is primarily that of the conflict between light and darkness that sets the boundaries for the struggle between good and evil in human life.

This is not abstract imagery. It requires an appreciation of how the symbolic sense of hymn and prayer texts is rooted in the realities of living by night and by day. This may help us to see what the significance of the blessing of the Paschal light might be. Some inspiration might be drawn from morning and evening hymns composed by Saint Ambrose of Milan. Noting the transition of the day from light to darkness and darkness to light, both morning and evening, these hymns looked to the light of Christ for consolation and hope.

---

23. See Robert Taft, *The Liturgy of the Hours in East and West* (Collegeville, Minn.: Liturgical Press, 1986), 174–76.

Table 6.1

Morning	Evening
Eternal maker of all things, who rules the night and day, and to time sets limits that you may relieve weariness. The nightly light separating night from night for wanderers, the herald of the day already sounds and calls forth the radiance of the sun. The morning star thus roused releases the heavens from darkness: At this (sound) every vagrant band leaves aside the way of causing harm. At this sound, the mariner gathers together his strength: At this sound, the very rock of the Church, singing, washes away fault. Let us therefore promptly arise: The cock arouses those who sleep, and noisily awakens the sleepy. The cock shames those who deny (the Lord). The cock singing, hope returns, to the sick health is restored, the sword of the robber is sheathed, faith is given back to the fallen. Jesus, look on the stumbling, and seeing us correct us; if you look, blemishes are removed, and by weeping fault is pardoned.	Already the fiery sun recedes: O Unity, blessed Trinity, eternal light, pour light into our hearts. In the morning with the song of praise, and in the evening we entreat you; May you deign that we suppliants may praise you among the heavenly hosts. To the Father and likewise to the Son, and to you, Holy Spirit, as it was, so may it be always glory for all time.

In Table 6.1, we give, side by side, one hymn for the morning and one for the evening.[24] In understanding these hymns, it may first be recalled that for the people of Milan and elsewhere, night was indeed a fearsome time. Travel or seafaring by night was difficult. Hence we see mention of the traveler who is happy to see the arrival of the morning light or of the mariner who gathers together his flagging strength when he sees the sun shine forth at the dawn of a new day. Journeying at night was difficult not only because of the lack of a guiding light but also because it was the time when marauders sought their prey. Thus Ambrose refers to the fact that vagrant bands disperse at break of day, leaving those on the road

---

24. The translation is the author's own.

or on the sea and those in their homes safer. Ambrose also takes note of the fact that those who are sick or moribund find the hours of the night most difficult and can even say that with the morning light health returns to the sick.

The images of the dark hours are to some extent used by Ambrose to refer to the sinful human condition and to the need that all have for cleansing and forgiveness. However, even if they have this metaphoric sense, they refer to real perils that people faced and from which they sought deliverance from God and through the light of Christ.

Today, these are still images wont to mark our fear of the night. Ironically, as remarked, in Western countries the fear of having people out during the night has led many churches to schedule the vigil at an early hour of the evening so that it is finished well before midnight. This itself is reminder enough of our fear of the darkness of night. It is still a time when thieves ply their trade. It is a time for gang fighting in many large cities. All night long one hears the wail of the sirens from the ambulances bringing the victims of violence to the emergency wards of hospitals. Sick people still feel at their lowest during the night, especially if they are deprived of sleep. They are without light, without company, and especially when deprived of medication they are at their lowest. Night indeed still stands for the ills, physical and moral, under which humanity labors. It is out of this somber shadow that people look to the light of Christ. Our present living can indeed provide the compositor of liturgical texts with many a metaphor of darkness.

In this dark we look to Christ. The tradition of our present texts is to look to him as the rising sun and to hail his victory over death and darkness. In line with the choice of the metaphor of *kenosis* we might instead remember him as the one who accompanies us into the night. This would not be simply to see him as the one who gives us a light by which to walk. It would be to hail him as the one who has chosen to be with us in the dread of the dark and to endure the terrors of the human night with us. It is such a love which animates and gives hope, even in darkness.

Blessing of the Baptismal Water

In the blessing of the baptismal water there is room for the evocation of images associated with the hymn in Philippians 2. More could be said of the descent of Christ into the waters of the River Jordan.

This has long been looked to as a paradigm for Christian baptism. On the one hand, it is the anointing of Christ with the Spirit which is also the anointing of those baptized in him. On the other hand, the waters were evoked in many a prayer as the very place of conflict between chaos and cosmos, between evil spirits and the Spirit of God. Christ too was celebrated as the fish who could swallow up the Leviathan of the deep. Indeed the Gospel itself tells us that at this moment Christ, without dissimulation, made himself one with sinners in seeking the baptism of John. What the imagery of self-emptying would allow would be to see Christ's own descent as an immersion with humanity into the agonies of dying and death and into the conflict between death and life. It is by enduring it that he overcomes it, and he still endures it today in his suffering members. It is in the faith and hope that he is with them that people can go forward, in their suffering and with their harsh memories, to the baptismal immersion with Christ and in Christ.

Eucharistic Prayer

In the prefaces of the Roman liturgy, old and current, the images of Abel, Abraham, and the Paschal Lamb serve to evoke the significance of Christ's Pasch. How they sound to a gathered assembly depends much on what scriptural background has been provided. The appropriation of these images might well take a new twist in the light of some of the interpretations suggested earlier in this work for the scriptural texts of the vigil.

In the one who is often called the "just Abel" we have the model of one who suffers for his righteousness at the hands of one who envies him his place with God. Through the story of Abel as a kind of universal story we can well see how to find Christ in all thus tortured. Of the binding of Isaac and the faith of Abraham, much has already been said. From the story of the Paschal Lamb, many things can carry over into the story of Christ who is one with his people in their agony and in the frail hope of their journey without maps. In the taking of the choice lamb for slaughter there is the offering by God of the choice Son who will be totally one with a suffering world, and indeed even one who stands in for the condemned or for those who are in the agony of the fear of death and subjection to darksome forces. There is the role of the Lamb's blood in protecting against death, and the eating of its flesh in a meal of fellowship taken in haste in order to flee the perils of destruction.

Of other prayers, the possibilities offered by the anaphora of Basil the Great should be noted because of the commanding place given in it to the image of *kenosis* taken from Philippians. It is true that use has been made of Eastern prayers, and even of this prayer, in the composition of new canons for the Roman Rite. These, however, pass over this aspect of Basil's text. Taking the lead from this image, the prayer speaks of the birth in humility by which the eternal Son took on the form of a slave and of his conformity to the body of our humiliation (by sin and death). In his own flesh he condemned sin in the flesh and walked among us as "citizen of this world." By means of the cross, he "descended into hell, that he might fill all things with himself, and loose the pains of death." To this, the prayer adds that he gave himself as a ransom to the death by which humans are held and that he was "sold under sin." There are of course also images of Christ's glory in this prayer and of his victory, but they emerge in their truth only because of the solid language that breaks open the full extent of his oneness with those who suffer sin and death in all their forms.

It is following on this imagery and after the invocation of the Spirit that the prayer introduces very concrete petitions for those whom the community could see around them or meet on their daily travels. There are the fainthearted, the scattered, the wanderers. There are the widows, the orphans, the sick, those facing trial, and the workers in the mines. There are those held in slavery and those who live in exile. All, it is claimed before God, who has already been reminded of the compassion shown in his Son, "need your great compassion." Not an awful lot of imagination is needed to update such petitions and to relate the needy of our age to the compassion shown in Christ's *kenosis*.

Conclusion

The scriptures cannot be appropriated unless they are prayed. The prayer that completes their hearing belongs to time and culture. Even as the choice of scriptural texts may change over time, so does the composition of prayers. The relation of a liturgy to the lives of people who see things in the light of events and social constructs affects what they find in both scripture and prayer text. In this chapter, the move from scripture to prayer within the liturgy has been examined for what it says of the interpretation of the scripture. In doing this, the particular setting of our own time was put to the fore. Having remarked how some particular root metaphor has seemed to prevail in other generations, it was asked what such image might serve today, at the cusp of another millennium, in this age of difficult and horrendous memory. With this, the effort to explore the interpretation of scripture as the Word of the Lord within the Church's liturgy has been brought to a conclusion.

The study first raised the issue within a contemporary context, this being followed by an inquiry into what might be called the life of a text within the life of a church. It then asked how may a community respect the original text even as it knows it is appropriating it in new ways. Next, the relation of interpretation to the historical and cultural context of the people was examined. Finally, we looked at the appropriation of biblical texts and images that is achieved through liturgical prayer. Throughout, the work has drawn on specific examples in order to avoid a purely speculative foray. The final chapters make specific recommendations of ways in which the image of divine *kenosis* may infuse our liturgies in these millennial days, as we look in faith to Christ among the weak of the earth.

Index